PAUL —

THANKS SO MUCH FOR

YOUR HELP.

I'M NOW WRITING A 2ND

BOOK - ABOUT MY "ADVENTURE" -

THE 4 YEARS AFTER MY

BRAIN INJURY.

Mike  1/28/13

# Spiritual Capitalism

Radical Transformation into Quantum Performance

Forget Every Rule You've Ever Been Taught

## Michael E. Hendren

Published by

Newhouse Books

ISBN 978-0-9795466-0-0

*This book is dedicated to my mom and dad, Josephine (Doll) and Coy.*

*My childhood home in Tennessee.*

# The Spiritual Capitalist, Inc.

Dear Stakeholder:

Thank you for purchasing my book. It can change your life.

Despite a horrific start in my life, I have been able to accomplish a great deal professionally while making a fortune and transforming many lives. I want to share with you the keys to my success. They are embodied in what I call Spiritual Capitalism, a combination of business acumen and spiritual love.

This philosophy is about coming from a place of love in the truest and strongest sense. It can transform you and your employees while allowing you to enrich your soul.

It is based on the belief that:

1.  Executives have a sacred responsibility to ensure their employees and companies realize their true professional and personal potential.

2.  This can be accomplished by blending the art and science of management into a transcendent level of leadership that transforms employees and companies and generates a quantum level of corporate financial performance.

3.  By managing with the intellect and power of the mind and leading with the heart through the transformative power of love, we can take our employees, our companies, and ourselves to that ultimate level of self-actualization.

Understand this is a radical philosophy, not for the faint of heart, and has, as its foundation, what some would call a maverick orientation. Contrarians are those who win big, knowing that the only way to transcend the norm is to do things differently. They think in quantum rather than linear terms that expand the mind into true possibility thinking. I am a contrarian. We'll be talking about a contrarian approach to business that has a unique intellectual, emotional, and spiritual energy.

My career was characterized by doing things differently and generating results beyond all expectations. I learned that one of the great pleasures in life is accomplishing what others think impossible. By adopting the Spiritual Capitalist philosophy, I know you can take your professional and personal life into a whole new dimension of deep intrinsic fulfillment.


Warmest personal regards,


Michael E. Hendren

# ACKNOWLEDGMENTS

Writing a first book is quite an experience.

It's an exhilarating, frustrating, satisfying, excruciating, and ultimately transforming process.

Since mine was based on a radical and unorthodox approach that goes against the traditional way of business thought, it was particularly important to get people around me who supported my goal in writing this book.

I knew I could provide people a guide to a joyful professional experience that also happened to result in extraordinary corporate financial performance. And, as I discussed with my minister and theology teachers, it could serve as a spiritual mission for me in this phase of my life.

Selling businesspeople on the transcendent power of spiritual love in terms of both the work environment dynamics and the financial return is an interesting proposition. I had the track record to prove this compelling concept, but articulating my beliefs in an invigorating and utilitarian book was a challenging objective.

Luckily, I had a cast of characters in my life that provided me the impetus and support I needed to make my dream a reality.

My mother, Josephine (Doll), and sisters, Barbara, and Heather, provided unconditional love, a very important factor in a life that began with poverty and abuse.

My children, Stacey, Amy, Russell, Sam, and David, kept me going throughout the ups and downs of life. As a father, I want them to know who I was, who I am, and who I always prayed I would be. I want to leave them a legacy they can feel good about. God knows I made more than my share of mistakes. I just hope that, after I'm long gone, this book will speak to the essence of my spirit.

Many mentors along the way—in particular, Coach Bob Miller, Dave Fuller, Jerry Miller, Mike Hayden, Bob Cherry, Dr. Ossama Hassenein, Mory Ejabat, and Dr. Alan Walker—gave me the freedom, support, and love to do my thing.

In terms of the hard work necessary to get this book written, my eternal gratitude to Fawn Germer, who provided invaluable guidance; Linda Lindsay, my precious sister; and Eric Brown, my main assistant on this project. Dr. Dan Ash, my spiritual mentor, demanded of me that I write this book as a spiritual mission.

Last, I feel that God has given me grace throughout my life. If I can promote spiritual love throughout the world of business, maybe I'll get a few brownie points.

# TABLE OF CONTENTS

# INTRODUCTION
## SPIRITUAL CAPITALISM

Spiritual Capitalism is the business philosophy that took me from a childhood of horrific abuse and poverty to becoming one of America's most successful and highest-paid business executives.

I say this not to gain your sympathy or impress you but to underscore the power of this rather radical approach to the business world. I grew up in a rural town of 113 people in Atoka, Tennessee. We lived in a house with no electricity, running water, or sanitation facilities, and I began working in the cotton fields at age 6. It was a suffocating environment for a child, and I lived in fear of being beaten to death. My dad finally killed himself, and my mom worked on an assembly line stuffing Kleenex boxes for more than thirty years. So much for my "pedigree."

So when I tell you that if I could go from where I started in life to the pinnacle of professional and financial achievement, you can, too, it's not an empty cliché but a profound truth. The issues, principles, managerial practices, and real-world examples I'll be discussing with you comprise the same approach I've used throughout my career. This approach is responsible for one of my greatest joys—the lives I've transformed. It has created many multimillionaires who are not only exceptionally successful executives but also leaders focused on ensuring their people and companies realize their true potential.

I wish I had the time and space to talk about the countless stories of all those with whom I've had the opportunity to come in contact over the years and to experience with them their transformation. All they needed was someone to see their potential, someone who demanded they be all they could be, and someone to give them the unconditional love we humans need to take us on the road to self-actualization.

Although Spiritual Capitalism has universal application, its most significant value is the power it creates in generating dramatic corporate growth. I experienced this throughout my career. My last company, Ascend Communications, was defined at the time by industry analysts as the fastest-growing enterprise in the history of American business. In particular, managerial disciplines we'll discuss—such as vision, high-performance culture, quantum goal setting, quantum sales performance, relationship selling, creating the right team, empowerment, and ownership—all center on taking companies to a level of growth far beyond any traditional standards.

I was called a maverick and contrarian in my corporate life, terms that I view as complimentary. I learned an early lesson in my career, a lesson that is invaluable if you want to ascend to what I call the quantum level of performance. In the dictionary, the term "quantum" refers to a sudden and extensive change into a different sphere of magnitude. It expresses the potential a company has to generate financial performance far beyond any traditional norms.

The fundamental truth is that if you want to transcend the norm, you must do things in a compellingly different manner. Spiritual Capitalism can guide you on an exciting and fulfilling contrarian path that has an impeccable track record. It's not a theory with little practical application, and I'm not an academician, a consultant, or one of those "motivational" speakers with no meat in his résumé. Progressive and successful companies such as Southwest Airlines, Best Buy, Virgin, Campbell Soup, Trammell Crow, Wal-Mart (particularly when Sam Walton built it), and IBM during its turnaround have used the fundamental principles embodied in the Spiritual Capitalism philosophy.

> *A 1999 issue of U.S. News & World Report reveals "in the past decade, more than 300 titles on workplace spirituality—from Jesus CEO to The Tao of Leadership—have flooded the bookstores.... Indeed, 30 MBA programs now offer courses on this issue. It is also the focus of the current issue of the 'Harvard School Bulletin.' You see examples of this focus on the corporate soul in the boardroom and company lunchroom, at management conferences, and in the studies of management consulting firms."*

My track record with small, medium, and large companies operating in domestic and international markets—and as a successful corporate turnaround specialist—validates the practice of Spiritual Capitalism. It came to full fruition with Ascend Communications.

When I arrived, Ascend was a struggling $12 million company with its primary competitors generating $10 billion to $40 billion in sales. Over a six-year period, we grew annual revenues to almost $1.6 billion, increased our staff from 30 to 3,000 employees, ran the company at an operating margin of 25%, and created a market value of $24 billion. In my position as executive vice president responsible for sales, worldwide field operations, and business development, this old cotton-picking country boy wound up making over $1 million a ***month*** (and that's not a typo).

Over the years, I had a number of business executives recommend that I write about what they described as the "elegantly unorthodox" philosophy, strategy, and operational tactics I've used so successfully in my career.

When I visited bookstores, I noticed that most of the business books were written by consultants or academicians with no substantial real-world business experience. A few were written by CEOs of giant Fortune 500 companies who do not connect with your average CEO, vice president, or departmental manager who wants and needs a fresh perspective. These writers seemed to lack a real understanding and empathy for the frontline managers who don't care about some esoteric theoretical approach to business that has nothing to do with their everyday challenges.

I presented what would become the outline for this book several years ago in Arizona to a large group of executives. The response was overwhelming. I was even offered the opportunity to run a $40 billion operation that evening. I knew then my message was radical and refreshing and would resonate strongly with the majority of the American workforce, the people trapped in the regressive traditional business model that leaves them unfulfilled, underperforming, and unaware of their true potential.

## THE POWER OF LOVE

When people ask how I was able to experience my amazing journey and transformation, I like to ask them a few questions. What touches us deeply? What moves us to act from our Higher Self? What is the most important value in our lives?

What motivates us like nothing else?

The real motivator, the most important dynamic in our personal and professional lives, is a strong form of spiritual love.

> *The Gallup Organization found that 95% of us say we believe in God or a "universal spirit." Some 48% report that they talked about their faith at work–that day*

But we tend to compartmentalize our lives into business and personal, work and play. As Richard Branson of Virgin likes to point out, life is life. A recent Gallup survey revealed the vast majority of us believe in a spiritual dimension to life. So why not use the power of spiritual love in our professional lives?

The fundamental premise of Spiritual Capitalism is that a spiritual perspective in our professional life—based on the type of spiritual love I'll be discussing with you—not only brings joy and fulfillment into the work environment but can be the most potent factor in generating phenomenal corporate performance.

The type of love I'm referring to is an invigorating, demanding, and compassionate form of spiritual love that:

- Creates a powerful and intimate dynamic within your team
- Challenges you to redefine possibility thinking
- Demands a commitment to a new vision of achievement
- Provides a culture of actualization for you, your teammates, and your company
- Generates breathtaking performance.

And the absolutely most loving thing you can do in business is to take yourself, your teammates, your company, and its stakeholders on the journey of transformation to a performance level in which the ultimate financial and psychological rewards are experienced.

## THE SPIRITUAL CAPITALIST

The Spiritual Capitalist approach to business offers the following benefits:

- Guides businesses and individuals to an optimal level of performance
- Provides a culturally rich and rewarding work environment
- Presents a path of transformation to professional and personal self-actualization
- Demonstrates how work can enhance the meaning of one's life
- Acknowledges the individual's spirituality.

It is about managing with the head and leading with the heart. You use the intellect and power of the mind with the uniquely transformative power of love. It's very different from what I call the Traditional Regressive business model. The following chart contrasts these two models:

| TRADITIONAL REGRESSIVE | SPIRITUAL CAPITALIST |
|---|---|
| Control | Empowerment |
| Shallow Leadership | Transformation |
| Frowns a Lot | Smiles a Lot |
| Policy Manuals | Freedom |
| Rules | Creativity |
| Politics | Love |
| Distrust | Love |
| Hatred | Love |
| Fear | Love |
| E-mail | Talking |
| Thinks Small | Thinks Large |
| Bureaucratic | Extemporaneous |
| Superficial | Humanistic |
| Looks Out for Me | Looks Out for Them |
| Boring | Fun |
| Suffocating | Breathtaking |
| Insecure | Courageous |
| Timid | Bold |
| Questionable Ethics | Internal Moral Compass |
| 65 Hours per Week | 35 Hours per Week |
| Marginal Performance | Quantum Performance |
| Sullen Employees | Inspired Employees |
| Excuses | Total Accountability |
| BS, BS, BS | Truth |
| Self-limiting | Self-actualizing |
| Asleep | Awakened |
| Disgruntled Shareholders | Ecstatic Shareholders |
| Suffers in Darkness | Thrives in the Light of Love |

When I present this contrast in my talks on Spiritual Capitalism, the delineation really hits home with the audience. The typical comment is something like, "Wow, that's the way we operate." And: "Until I saw this, I didn't know there was an alternative, particularly one so stimulating with such a powerful track record."

## SELF-ACTUALIZATION

Recent surveys indicate more than 80% of our workforce detest their jobs and hate going to work. This is a staggering statistic and a horrible indictment of the Traditional Regressive approach.

The problem is reflected in Abraham Maslow's famous Hierarchy of Needs. The Traditional Regressive culture addresses only the bottom two levels of the pyramid, physiological and safety. A culture of Spiritual Capitalism moves the individual up through the social needs of belonging and love into the self-esteem stage and ultimately to the point of self-actualization, where true potential is realized and quantum performance is achieved.

It looks something like this:

## QUANTUM PERFORMANCE

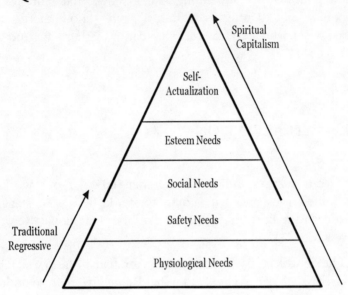

## ONLY TWO BASICS

I'd like you to understand this powerful truth fully. When people ask me what factors must a company have to perform financially at such a high level, they're a bit stunned by the simplicity of my answer.

If you're in a good market and have a competitive product, then your company can achieve what you never dreamed possible. With these two requirements met, any issues regarding company, market, and product positioning have been addressed. Given these two fundamentals, the key variables leading to quantum performance are superb leadership and management execution. That's it.

Many companies have competitive products addressing a good market. So why aren't they enjoying the joy and rewards of outstanding performance? The answer is they are stuck, drowning, or dying in the Traditional Regressive business model. They need to understand that a contrarian approach instead of the "norm" is the critical variable.

Spiritual Capitalism is the contrarian approach that's required for transformation. This philosophy couples the spiritual (empowerment, liberation, transformation) with capitalism (quantum performance, productivity, astute financial management).

## THE TEN COMMANDMENTS OF SPIRITUAL CAPITALISM

My book focuses on the Ten Commandments of Spiritual Capitalism:

I. **Define Business as a Spiritual Experience**—Practice a strong, demanding, and challenging love as the ultimate motivator and path to self-actualization for yourself, your team, and your company.

II. **Don't Shrink or Play Small in This World**—Truly understand, at a deep spiritual level, the power and presence you have to realize fulfillment in your personal and professional life.

III. **Dare to Love and the Numbers Will Follow**—Use the head and heart in achieving a breakthrough level of quantum performance that few ever experience.

IV. **Embrace Leadership as a Sacred Responsibility**—Accept the absolute responsibility of leadership to take your people to a place they never could have imagined.

V. **Develop Management into an Art**—Apply grace, elegance, and efficacy.

VI.  **Empower Them with Ownership**—Make the psychological, operational, and financial investment, then watch the ROI grow exponentially.

VII.  **Transcend to the Higher Level**—No excuses, no politics, no avoiding accountability, no b.s. – just extraordinary performance in an invigorating and supportive environment.

VIII.  **Don't Take It All So Seriously**—This paradox actually liberates potential.

IX.  **Count Your Blessings**—Put everything in perspective while constructing a foundation of gratitude.

X.  **The Truth Will Set You Free**—Within a strong spiritual love, truth provides the path to both personal and professional transcendence while elevating work into a journey that enhances the meaning of one's life.

My objective in this introduction has been to provide you a general overview of Spiritual Capitalism.

Throughout the book, I'll discuss many real-world examples of breakthrough approaches used in fueling stunning performances. I'm honored to be your guide on this road to transformation. It's a journey that enriches the mind and venerates the soul.

# CHAPTER 1

## DEFINE BUSINESS AS
## A SPIRITUAL EXPERIENCE

*"When you are born, your work is placed in the heart."*
*Kahlil Gibran*

What comes to mind when you think of business and spirituality in the same context? Religion in the workplace? Prayer meetings in the break room? Passing out Bibles? If you are like many traditional business leaders I know, you may think spirituality in business is like oil and water—they don't mix.

I have respect for all religious practices. When I refer to spirituality, I'm talking about what I consider a deeper and more universal expression of human life. All of us, regardless of religious orientation, possess an innate spiritual dimension. I've studied theology all my life and am currently a theology major at our local university. I've come to believe spirituality is about growth and transformation, in spiritual terms rebirth. It's about going deep within to become what you were designed to be. The spiritual dimension within demands that you come from your Higher Self and leads us, through conscious effort and heightened awareness, to feel a genuine love for others.

It shows up in the business world in terms of how you care for and respect your employees. It's about managing with your head but leading with your heart. The word "heart" is referred to in the Holy Scriptures more than 500 times and is defined as the center of the spiritual self. As a leader, you must believe in your employees more than they believe in themselves and be committed to facilitating their growth. In my experience, these actions allow you to create a stimulating and fulfilling work environment, which can create phenomenal business success.

Spirituality can get you to a point of emotional valor, a dignity and elegance of character that occurs when your outer actions in this world align with your inner spiritual journey. Your actions serve to build your relationship with Divinity, connecting the material and spiritual worlds.

As mentioned in the introduction, I've had a lot of people ask how I was able to come from my troubled background to the level of professional and financial achievement with which I am blessed. People want to know what the real key was.

It's not your childhood. It's not your parents. It's not your education.

It's not cajoling. It's not intimidating. It's not soliciting. It's not screaming. It's not threatening.

It's not a great business plan. It's not the product. It's not the marketing. It's not endless meetings and e-mails. It's not endless "pep talks." It's not the money.

The real motivator, the most powerful dynamic in life and business, is a strong form of spiritual love. In my studies of the great spiritual masters of Christianity, Islam, Buddhism, Hinduism, and Judaism, there is one common denominator. The single thread connecting all of these masters is that spirituality and love can and should coexist in all aspects of our lives.

The fundamental premise of Spiritual Capitalism is that spirituality not only brings peace, harmony, and joy to the office, it can be the most potent factor in superior financial performance.

When you come from a spiritual perspective, all your actions are guided by a strong, caring, tough, and demanding multidimensional managerial compass. And the ultimate act of love is taking yourself, your team, and your company to a place where the real potential is realized—that level of self-actualization at the top of Maslow's pyramid.

## THE SPIRITUAL CAPITALIST PERSPECTIVE

The inherent genius in the Spiritual Capitalist's foundation of spirituality—unlike traditional motivational efforts—is that you tap into that place deep within the human heart that responds like nothing else. It creates and sustains a strong emotional energy that's contagious.

If your people know they are loved and respected, that you have their best interest at heart, and there are no hidden agendas, they focus on going there with you and making it happen for you. Acts of tough love, constructive confrontation, not accepting the unacceptable, demanding they reach their true potential, and relieving those who don't fit into your high-performance culture are, in fact, acts of love.

In *The Road Less Traveled*, M. Scott Peck defines love as "the extending of oneself to promote the spiritual growth of another." Once this bond is established, the leader is given amazing power and flexibility to take people where they really want to be.

Love is integral to the definition of spirituality. As we use spirituality to embrace our people and accept a sacred responsibility to guide them to a place of self-actualization, we liberate ourselves and our companies. I believe spirituality flows through people, through you and me—like a delicate breeze of grace, guiding us through love to a higher place personally and professionally.

Before I talk more about Spiritual Capitalism and the value of defining business as a spiritual experience, I'd like to share a story with you.

I did a business deal with the Trammell Crow Company in Dallas, the largest commercial real estate company in the U. S. and probably the world. I met Mr. Crow who, from humble beginnings, built an empire. He had a warm and gentle way and a powerfully understated presence. One of his staff told me the Harvard Business School once asked him to speak to their graduating students. He talked to them in general terms about strategic and tactical issues. During the Q and A, someone asked him to define the single most important factor in building his incredibly successful company.

After a long pause, Mr. Crow answered simply, "Unconditional love." He then walked off the stage.

Mr. Crow knew the value of seeing business as a spiritual experience based on the unique power of love. I hope those Harvard graduates, with all their training in various management disciplines, truly understood and took in this incomparable principle in building great companies.

## THE BEGINNING

How did I come to understand spirituality as fundamental to a successful business philosophy?

Years ago, I lived in Laguna Beach, California, working with Honeywell's computer division. I loved the beach, the ocean, and just about everything in California. I was California all the way—a long-haired surfer dude who also happened to be a superstar salesman making great money and enjoying life big time.

Our VP in Detroit called and said he was looking for a new manager for one of the field offices. "Mike, you'll be a fantastic leader. This is a great opportunity for you." As he continued stroking me, my gut told me there must be a catch. So I asked where he wanted to send me. He mumbled, "St. Louis." As a lover of the beach and the sunny California climate, I had visions of freezing to death. Then I asked him where St. Louis stood in the rankings against our other field offices. He mumbled again, "Last."

My first reaction was to turn him down. After all, I was making lots of money, enjoying life, and working 25 hours a week. Why would I want the headaches and responsibility of management? It was completely unappealing to me at the time. Then I thought about how the spiritual principles I had been using allowed me to create strong relationships with clients and coworkers. People were enthusiastic about helping me create success. Maybe I already was a leader. Maybe I did not realize how the power of Spiritual Capitalism could transform the lives of others. It was worth exploring, so I decided to check things out in St. Louis.

On the flight to meet the team there, I wrestled with the whole idea of uprooting myself and becoming a manager. I could not imagine myself ordering other people around and being responsible for their performance. As a salesperson, I was comfortable having a number on my head and creating strong, caring relationships that brought me exceptional success. It's a thrilling profession. Success and failure are all up to you. The idea of bringing others into the equation caused me concern.

When I arrived at the St. Louis office, the team didn't exactly welcome me with open arms. Their expressions seemed to say, "Who is this guy from California who looks more like a surfer than a businessman?" and "Why should we listen to him?"

We sat down to discuss their operation and obstacles that kept them in last place among our other offices. I could see fear in their eyes, a lack of belief in themselves and their team, a lack of unity, and a lack of heart. They looked downtrodden and seemed desperate for someone to come and save them, to "get them out alive." I literally felt sorry for them. Then an amazing thing happened.

As I looked at them, I felt what can only be described as love surging in my heart. I knew I could transform them and take them to a place they had never been. A voice inside me said, "Let's go for it." And I did.

I met with each member of the team and had a heart-to-heart talk about how we were going to turn the business around. I showed them how to create relationships and build them for the long term. I taught them how to close the deal and reach goals they never thought possible. I demonstrated my belief in them, and at that time I believed in them more than they believed in themselves. Our office went from worst to first in less than a year. All of our lives were changed in the process.

I was then asked to take over a larger regional operation in another city. My team held a fabulous going-away party for me. As we said our goodbyes, there was not a dry eye in the entire place. The whole environment was saturated with a spiritual presence.

It was through this experience and my own personal transformation that Spiritual Capitalism was born.

## THE SPIRITUAL CAPITALIST APPROACH

Spiritual Capitalism integrates the cognitive left brain with the creative right brain, using the intellect of the mind with the transformative power of the heart. It's a contrarian approach that's centered on an authentic feeling of love for yourself, others, and your company. It will liberate those of you who think your religious principles might conflict with the tough decisions the successful capitalists must face each day.

The Spiritual Capitalist, in sharp contrast to the traditional approach, asks these types of provocative and challenging questions in developing managerial policies:

1.  Why not release people who are underperforming quickly in a graceful and compassionate manner, particularly since they are caught up in their own personal purgatory because of this self-knowledge?

2.  Why should a manager rush out to hire bodies because he just got a budget approval, when the hiring act has such a profound effect on the company and the individual?

3.  Why settle for traditional bottoms-up forecasting methods with their built-in hedge factors rather than truly challenge the team with a top-down quantum goal-setting process that reaches for greatness?

4.  Why not spread stock options among all employees? Why not realize the statement that makes and the motivation it provides throughout your company, rather than allowing greed to limit this benefit to senior executives?

5.  Why not truly practice empowerment and ownership rather than let micromanagement hold your people back?

6.  Why not have a management process that's lean and responsive instead of a bureaucratic block that drives your people nuts?

7.  Why not have the courage to constructively confront the unacceptable real-time rather than constantly "rationalizing"?

8.  Why burden your people with hundreds of e-mails each week that take all that time to compose, interpret, and answer, when other means of communication are more timely, precise, personal, and less expensive?

9. Why inflict the brain damage of the annual performance review when the good manager knows his people?

10. Why bug your people about inconsequential expenses when managing headcount and productivity is the ballgame in terms of profitability?

We'll use this type of questioning as our guide in discussing powerful and creative approaches to the many real-world examples of managerial application defined throughout the book.

## THERE IS ANOTHER WAY

I know a lot of business leaders get uncomfortable when talking about things like love and joy in the workplace. But I ask my skeptics, "Do you want to keep doing things the way you're doing them? Are you successful? Are you having fun? Are you making big money? Are your company's revenues and profits growing exponentially?"

The outmoded business practices of the past—top-heavy management, greed at the helm, an employees-be-damned attitude, a self-interest focus in management—just don't cut it anymore. I've had amazing financial results with Spiritual Capitalism. I've also had a lot of fun in the process while making a fortune for my team, my companies, and myself.

The vast majority of people in business are struggling to build successful companies in environments that deplete rather than nurture. There's a lack of joy, fun, and esprit de corps. Few will ever actualize their true potential. This is the primary reason why those 80% of people hate their jobs and hate to go to work.

What if I told you…

- You can love going to work.

- You can love those you work with.

- You can maximize your earnings.

- You can optimize your company's performance.

- You can work fewer hours, create a balanced life, and spend quality time with your kids.

- You can laugh a lot.

- You can throw away the policy manuals.

- You can experience frequent, overwhelming episodes of appreciation.

- Office politics will become a distant memory.

- You can lose the ability to worry.

- You can grow professionally and spiritually— exponentially.

- You can develop an uncontrollable urge to extend love to others as well as receive more love yourself.

You can.

A spiritual business perspective involves a conscious choice, an attitude to work with others and your company at a higher level of strength, joy, and love. It represents an expansion of consciousness allowing you to operate in a new state of awareness.

People ask, "What's the downside? What do I risk losing?" The answers to those questions are the very factors that tie you in and deny liberation of true potential. With this new philosophical perspective, you will leave behind:

- A constant funk about work.

- Conflict with your team members.

- A lack of individual and collective self-confidence.

- The suffocating habit of thinking small.

- Individual and collective underperformance.

- Long, ridiculous hours at work.

- Extreme stress that provides you things like constant headaches, ulcers, heart attacks, impotency, and ultimately death.

- Fear.

- Backstabbing.

- Lowball compensation.

- Estrangement from your family due to your long hours, fear, and self defeating, neurotic, compulsive obsession with work.

Instead of going through your workday in a mechanical, semiconscious state driven by a "this is the way I always did it" mind-set (typically driven by a semineurotic perspective on business and life), you break free. You awaken to the higher ground of love and discover what it's all about. You start giving your work, your life, and the world the absolute best you have to offer. You grasp that work can play a role in your spiritual journey. It can in fact enhance the meaning and purpose of your life.

And you understand that a spiritual perspective based on a strong and powerful love is key to realizing some of the compelling benefits of the Spiritual Capitalist approach:

- A universal managerial and leadership philosophy

- Quantum financial performance

- Integrity

- Joy in your work

- Transformation

- Actualization—for you, others, your team, and your company.

## IT WORKS

When I began speaking about Spiritual Capitalism to other business executives I could see some initial skepticism. To address their concern, I would talk about my track record with small, medium, and large companies and successful corporate turnarounds. I'd then show them some numbers that reflected the type of quantum performance possible with this contrarian business philosophy.

My last professional position was with Ascend Communications as executive vice president of worldwide field operations (and designated "spiritual leader"). It was a small, struggling company manufacturing telecom-munications and networking equipment that was generating only $12 million in annual sales. Our competitors ranged in size from $10 billion to $40 billion!

Most companies talk about growing maybe 20% a year, but I wanted us to at least triple in size. That's what I call quantum performance. "Quantum" is the term I use frequently because it represents improvement on an order of magnitude greater than any kind of traditional standards.

I analyzed our market in terms of growth, share, and positioning. I reviewed our competition's strengths, weaknesses, and employee productivity. I decided how to optimize our organization and the financial investment I could make to achieve the sales growth while maintaining a 25% pretax operating margin.

I knew it was possible and decided it was unacceptable to fail. I've found that you get exactly what you demand—from yourself and from others. At the end of the year, our revenue was $37 million. Our team was incredibly proud of this achievement, particularly since most did not believe it was possible. They loved the rush of exceptional accomplishment, the money they'd earned, and the stock options I had awarded them. They now understood what I meant by quantum.

Every year after that, we achieved quantum performance. We kept growing dramatically and, five years later, we generated more than *$1 billion* in revenues while maintaining world-class profitability. Quantum performance? We had become one of the fastest-growing companies in American business history. We had expanded from 30 employees to 3,000 and created a market value of $24 billion. This extraordinary experience was driven by the force of Spiritual Capitalism.

During this time, I confirmed the universality of this business philosophy. I had initially run our North American business as we redefined the term "growth." Our sales had exploded to some $150 million per quarter. But our international business was stagnating at around $35 million per quarter.

Our guys in international always had the "answers" when questioned about this dramatic difference. "It's different in international." "Different countries." "Different cultures." "Different languages." "Different ways of doing business." But I'm thinking: Same market, same product, and same competition. And people are people.

So I took over our international business. I went to Hong Kong, Tokyo, China, England, France, Germany, and South America and shared the principles of Spiritual Capitalism with everyone. At each stop, I explained my philosophy of doing business and spent quality time answering questions and bonding. I then gave each manager a week to send me a tactical game plan that would achieve the quantum performance I expected.

Unfortunately, I had to fire our VPs in Germany and South Korea because they couldn't embrace this new way of doing business. I never risk a team's performance and welfare because of a marginal manager. I will explain later how firing can be done in a caring and compassionate manner. I included the VPs who did "get it" in our management process, inviting them to participate in a two-hour worldwide teleconference on Monday mornings, which tracked our business and resolved issues in real time.

I had simply implemented the different philosophical perspective of Spiritual Capitalism into our international operation. Within two quarters of this fundamental change, our international business was generating around $76 million per quarter and the people had been transformed in the process.

I used this same approach to transformation with my other companies, all with outstanding results.

Spiritual Capitalism is an empirical fact. It has proven itself as a powerful and replicable model that has worked in small and large companies without cultural, geographical, or language barriers. I used it with equal success in the U.S. and internationally. A number of high-profile business leaders such as Trammell Crow, Herb Kelleher, Sam Walton, Doug Conant, Lou Gerstner, and Richard Branson exemplify its principles.

## HOW IT LOOKS

There are a number of simple but powerful ways to demonstrate the tenets of Spiritual Capitalism in the office:

- You come from a place of empowerment versus control.

- You look your people in the eye and smile.

- You give them freedom versus policy manuals.

- You release their creativity instead of giving them a set of rules.

- You talk to them instead of at them or, even worse, use e-mail as your form of communication.

- You *really* listen to them.

- You look out for them instead of for yourself.

- You pick them up when they are down.

- You celebrate their victories.

- You make work fun and self-enhancing.

- You think big instead of small.

- You give them quantum goals and help them get there.

- You frequently underscore how much you care for them.

- You believe in them more than they believe in themselves.

- You take their breath away with your vision of possibilities.

Most important, you've raised your consciousness to a level where, no matter the issue, your actions are guided by the power of a tough, demanding, and empathetic form of love focused on growth and transformation.

This energizes a high-performance culture in which:

- Leadership is treated as a sacred responsibility.

- The people are invested in a compelling vision for the company.

- People think quantum rather than linear.

- People have great pride in their company.

- The unacceptable is not accepted.

- The transformative power of love is felt by the people.

- Psychological, operational, and financial ownership is the norm.

- All the BS is put aside in favor of high performance and accountability.

- There's a lot of laughter, smiles, lightness, and humor.

- A powerful emotional, intellectual, and spiritual energy is present.

## MAKING THE CHANGE

Too many companies are managed by boring men and women who create unproductive environments that their employees hate. Rules, regulations, policies, and paperwork dominate. Managers hide out in their offices avoiding contact with their people. Motivational attempts swing from pleading to intimidation. More time is spent administering performance reviews than truly getting to know people—their strengths and weaknesses, dreams, spirituality, and relationships with one another.

Most significant, the company has become spiritually bankrupt, with employees feeling a lack of love for themselves, their company, and one another. The company has lost its soul.

But when a leader incorporates spiritual principles into his managerial philosophy, amazing transformation can occur. This type of leader can take his people to a place they never dreamed possible. Spiritual principles with appropriate doses of tough love are blended to touch their hearts, minds, and souls. Employees are reoriented to a new vision of profound achievement. A picture is painted for them that shows exactly where they're going and how they're going to get there. Workers knows how they fit into the

> ### Spirituality at Work?
>
> *"If America's chief executives had tried any of this ten years ago, they probably would have inspired ridicule and maybe even ostracism. But today, a spiritual revival is sweeping across Corporate America as executives of all stripes are mixing mysticism into their management, importing into office corridors the lessons usually doled out in churches, temples, and mosques. Gone is the old taboo against talking about God at work."*
>
> *BusinessWeek*

big picture and what they need to do to ascend to a new level filled with pride and a genuine sense of accomplishment.

And, everyone knows he or she is loved.

They know because they are made to feel important. They are empowered for self-transcendence and know they will be cared for, protected, and respected. They get stock options in the company, receive exciting compensation plans whose benefits accelerate upon quantum achievement, and are offered genuine opportunities for growth. They're told they're loved and the depth of this commitment is followed up with action.

Once this new type of culture is created, a subtle dimension of spirituality evolves. Humor and lightness appear, followed by joy. People begin to care for one another and recognize a common purpose. They begin believing in themselves and an individual and collective self-confidence emerges. Revenues and profits soar with this new belief in team and self.

If you can get yourself into the humanistic, spiritual mind-set we've been discussing, you can achieve at a level you could have never envisioned. You must simply

> *"Many of today's employees, even though well compensated, report a feeling of incompleteness. Employees leave authentic spirituality and emotions at home, almost splitting themselves in two. They experience a feeling of uneasy bouncing back and forth depending on where they are, who they are with, and what time of day it is. Organizations demand more time, psychic energy, loyalty, and imagination from employees than ever before, but continue to treat them as if they were interchangeable parts. Contemporary organizations are efficient at meeting the material needs of their stakeholders, but often neglect those higher level needs that are more difficult to measure. These criticisms are frequently made by organizational theorists, sociologists, religionists, and employees themselves."*
>
> *Journal of Business Ethics, December 2003*

have the intelligence, insight, strength, and commitment to make the conscious choice to change into a Spiritual Capitalist. Throughout this book, I will act as teacher to provide you the fundamental knowledge for this transformation. I am honored to serve in this role and begin the journey with you.

It's a spiritually oriented path that few have taken in the business world. And yet we know that spiritual love continues to be the greatest motivator in growth and transformation.

When people are uncomfortable with their spirituality and fail to practice it in their professional lives, they lose the most powerful dynamic in exceptional performance, great teamwork, and self-transcendence. Though the path of spirituality meets resistance in the business world, it yields the greatest results and most satisfaction. Unfortunately, the typical mind-set in business follows a herd mentality, but people do not thrive in a herd.

No matter how you got into your position of leadership, I'm sure you aspire to go to a place where few have gone—to the top of the mountain, which is a quiet place within you. It's the self-knowledge that you attain with exceptional achievement, when you have touched lives deeply and you have realized your true potential, the level of self-actualization we've defined.

Ultimately, actualization is not a level on some hierarchy but a place in the heart. To get there, you dream, you dare, and you love. You can change your thinking from "what is wrong or missing" to a focus on spirituality and gratitude. You will realize that you have to move to a higher level of thinking and spiritual awareness. You will understand that the level of thinking that created your problems cannot be used to solve them.

## HOW YOU GET THERE

As I mentioned earlier, when people ask me what must be in place at a company before spectacular performance is possible, they're always surprised by the simple answer. If you're in a good market and have a competitive product, you can achieve quantum performance. Then it's all up to the quality of your leadership and management. It's that simple—and that challenging. And that's where the practice of Spiritual Capitalism can make such a dramatic difference.

Typically, in an underperforming company, a vacuum in leadership creates a crippling environment. Radical change requires serious self-analysis at such a company. The eight steps required to facilitate this include:

1. **Darkness**—Acknowledge that current operations arrest the potential of the people and company.

2. **The Cost**—Recognize that the status quo generates nothing but underachievement and lack of spirit.

3. **The Search**—Open up to new ways of thinking.

4. **Seize the Moment**—Know the time to act is now.

5. **Awareness**—Tune into a higher plane of consciousness that demands passion and excellence.

6. **Effort**—Aggressively define and attack key problems.

7. **Quantum Mind-set**—Have higher standards, higher goals, higher expectations.

8. **The Light**—Awaken to the reality of a stimulating and empowering spiritual love as the cornerstone of greatness.

If these steps are taken and someone steps up to become a real leader—looking at his position as having a sacred responsibility to those he leads—then the people are liberated by a culture that nurtures and supports them. Their self-defeating behavior is eradicated, and they move into their true selves.

The experience of work then becomes an avenue to enriching one's life and the essence of spirituality, growth, and transformation, is lived fully each day.

## Chapter Summary

- Spiritual Capitalism is about managing with the head and leading with the heart by integrating the power and intellect of the mind with the transformative power of love.

- Blending business life with spiritual life is key to generating quantum financial performance….Life is Life.

- What we've all been taught—the Traditional Regressive business model—has proven to be ineffectual and inhibits our spiritual growth.

- Benefits of Spiritual Capitalism include exceptional corporate performance, joy at work, transformation, integrity, and self-actualization.

- Spiritual Capitalism guides you into a powerful and paradigm-shifting business philosophy that offers a track record of extraordinary achievement and universal application.

P.S. I'm what my friends call a very amateur poet. But I love poetry because it's language from the heart. On the next page, I will leave you with one of my poems…

## Love

In the work place?

No way
Keep your distance
Don't get too close
You can't do that

That's what they say

But who are they?
And what do they know?
And how deeply do they feel?

In the field of battle
Our lives are linked
Our lights burning brightly
Into the heavens

We care for each other

We laugh together
Cry together
And hope together

We hurt together
Mourn together
And celebrate together

You can love and lead them to transcendence

Or manage them into mundaneness

What legacy will you leave?

A star shining brightly

Or the dull sound
Of a wasted journey

# CHAPTER 2

# DON'T SHRINK OR PLAY
# SMALL IN THIS WORLD

*"We are what we think. All that we are arises with our thoughts."*
*Buddha*

One of the most powerful speeches I've ever read is from Nelson Mandela's inauguration. Because he stayed true to his principles, he went to prison for 27 years before being released in 1990. He received constant beatings and torture from the prison guards. Through it all, he maintained his dignity and self-respect every second of the day. He refused to shrink or play small, even in such an intimidating and suffocating environment.

Over time, Mandela and his prison guards began to know and love each other. When he was finally released, those same guards who beat and tortured him said their good-byes with tears in their eyes.

Here's a section from the speech I love so much:

*Who am I to be brilliant?*
*Gorgeous, talented, and fabulous?*
*Actually, who are you not to be?*
*You are a child of God*

*Your playing small*
*Doesn't serve the world*

*There is nothing enlightened*
*About shrinking around others*

*We were born to make manifest*
*The glory of God that is within us*
*It's not just in some of us*

*It's in everyone*

*And as we let our own light shine*

*We unconsciously give other people*
*Permission to do the same*

*As we are liberated from our own fears,*
*Our presence automatically liberates others.*

I hope this takes your breath away as it does mine. My suggestion to you is to put it up on your wall. Its force is mighty. Nelson Mandela's moving inauguration speech can apply to everyone.

Its message centers on understanding our innate power to realize personal and professional fulfillment. Our playing small doesn't serve the world. As we let our light shine, we give others permission to do the same. As we are liberated from our own fears, our presence automatically liberates others.

One of our fundamental challenges is to liberate ourselves to this truth and develop the spiritual growth that goes hand in hand with professional development. We must confront our insecurities and step into the sphere of thinking big and playing large. Without this philosophical approach, exceptional performance and self-actualization in the business world are impossible. It takes courage and an absolute belief in self to put it all on the line. But the rewards can be enormous with this first step out of the incremental and into the world of quantum performance.

I am certainly not the smartest, smoothest, or best-raised person. Yet I've been blessed in a way that got me out of the cotton fields, created spectacular business success, and made me millions, while touching and transforming a lot of lives. This is what I want to share with you.

When people ask the key factors in my success, I point to thinking big, believing in myself, and really loving people. In particular, thinking big is the license to accomplish great things. Yet most people do not engage themselves in a vision that takes them to another level. You must do this if you hope to achieve quantum performance. THINK BIG!!!! Look at Mandela's words again. Then commit yourself to a whole new vision of possibility.

## YOUR PEOPLE ARE THE ULTIMATE DIFFERENTIATOR

In every market, a number of companies have competitive products that satisfy a need of their target customer. It is the innate way of a capitalistic system. Different salespeople with different companies put different spins on different products— and at the end of the day they are all comparable and all will do the job.

Consequently, *people and relationships*—not products—are the ultimate differentiator in a company's success. This is where Mandela's words become so compelling because most people fail to see themselves in grand spiritual terms. If they decide to take this in, not to shrink but to think big and play large, their whole mind-set changes.

The self-confidence this perspective generates reflects itself in the ability to create strong positive relationships with others and moves the individual to another level of competency in his or her work. The differentiator for the company thus becomes the strength of its people in all aspects of its operation.

## THE INNER CRITIC

What stops us from being all that we can be? We've had a lot of stuff poured into us. From childhood to present day, everyone has gone through various degrees of traumatic events. That seems to be a part of the deal. Then we see the therapists, believe we're irrevocably programmed, and kind of resign ourselves to self-defeating behavior.

It shows up as that little negative, neurotic voice in your head. You know the one—we all have it in some form or fashion. It's what the psychologist calls your inner critic.

It says you can't do something, you'd better look at the policy manual before just going with your gut, you better hope the boss doesn't yell at you. It says, "You'll never be able to make these goals," " You better check those 100 e-mails tonight before going to bed instead of making love to your wife," " You have to work 60 hours a week to keep your job and get ahead," "You better get x, y, and z done before HR gets on your case," "You could lose a few pounds," and "This presentation to the board is life and death," ad nauseam.

Anyone out there hearing this?

That inner critic says you can't tell someone you love him or her in the workplace. It says you need to look like you are always working furiously hard. It makes you choose working on finishing a report rather than going to your son's soccer game. It tells you to write another cover-your-ass memo, follow policy, stick to procedures, blah, blah, blah—whatever.

We all have our baggage, and some of us are scarred for life. But, we can reframe many of the traumatic events, analyzing them at a deeper level to search for the positives, the upsides, and the blessings in disguise. Those cotton fields in Tennessee where I grew up sure gave me a lot of motivation. I knew I wasn't going to make it in a career as a cotton picker. I didn't even know if I was going to get out of there alive.

Over the years, I've discovered hidden blessings in that horrific experience. It seems that in my case, God's grace evened things out in my life. And for that, I am extremely grateful. I know without a doubt, that without those life experiences, I would not be the man I am, nor would I have had the professional success with which I was blessed.

Once you truly integrate the essence of Mandela's word, you'll find your inner critic is quieter and that, with a sense of humor and gentle perspective, you can actually make it just another dimension of your psyche.

## LIBERATION

There simply comes a point when you have to turn off that poisonous inner voice. It's easier than you think once you commit yourself to it. Brain research gives us empirical evidence that the more we act a certain way—positive, negative, happy, sad—the more the behavior gets ingrained in our brain circuitry.

Experimenting with new behaviors eventually triggers in our brains the neural connections necessary for genuine change to occur. Know and believe that it is your decision, second by second, to be that person you've defined as your aspiration.

Watch your thoughts, and when you catch yourself in a negative mode, you must challenge it with a more constructive and positive approach. A simple approach can override destructive negative thinking. Psychologists call it cognitive therapy, and there are a lot of good books on it.

You never completely get rid of that negative voice, but you can make friends with it, recognize what's behind it, and use it to propel yourself forward. After a while, that negative neurotic inner voice tones down drastically—and you finally become the brilliant, beautiful, intelligent, successful, lovable person you were designed to be.

## OUR SEARCH FOR SPIRITUALITY

The leading-edge thinking in transpersonal psychology acknowledges that spiritual and transcendent needs are intrinsic to human nature and that satisfying these needs is the right and need of every individual. Consciousness was on the leading edge of psychotherapy in the 1990s. Today it is spirituality. We want to live a more peaceful, happy, and fulfilled life in harmony with the Divine. This requires a readiness to understand our own deeply spiritual nature.

Thinking big isn't just about increasing profits by 40%. It's also believing that your employees are part of the Divine and encouraging them to tap into this belief system whereby they truly KNOW they have the power to think big.

The problem is that the models we have used are weak, intellectual constructs that underestimate the human potential. There is a universal nature to the human spiritual experience. It is at this level that humans can experience their uniqueness and their ability to transcend and to participate in the cosmos on an almost mystical level.

## THE SPIRITUAL PERSPECTIVE

The Spiritual Capitalist thinks and plays large and urges the people around her to do the same. The Spiritual Capitalist shows them how to achieve quantum results. She becomes the model for her people. This is the most legitimate and instructive approach to leading others toward this concept. The people "buy into it" because her genuineness and efficacy moves them.

I believe we are ultimately spiritual beings on some grand adventure here on earth. If we were chosen for this experience, we indeed are children of God. Once you take that in, in a deep and profound way, you recognize that you were designed to be brilliant, gorgeous, talented, and powerful. When you look at yourself from this perspective, the world changes.

You begin to look at everything around you differently. You quit the shrinking and playing small dance because it does not serve you or our world. You go from the dark of your shackles to the light of this liberating truth. Know the glory of God is within you, or you wouldn't be here. You can take that little speck of Spirit born within you and slay the fiercest dragon, or you can walk on water.

This spiritual path of light liberates us from our fears and instills in us the qualities we need for this journey. When we decide to shine our light brightly and work to our true potential, we inspire others to the same path. That is the core of Spiritual Capitalism and the epitome of leadership.

## FAITH

Faith gives the license and energy to think big. It requires walking —and leaping—into the unknown. If you're going to apply the spiritual capitalist principle of thinking big, that means doing things differently. It's taking the road less traveled.

I have no interest in telling you what religion to practice or how to practice it. But I am urging you to stop restricting your faith and spirituality into something you think about and act on just at home and possibly at church. Bring it with you to work.

You can make the conscious decision to believe or not. You can make the decision to have faith or not. I ask myself questions such as did all of this happen by accident? Earth—*an accident?* Nature—*an accident?* Human life—*an accident?* The planets and stars—*accidents?* Or is there a majestic, mysterious, intelligent force behind all of this? Do you think it all just happened, or did something start all of this? Are we alone, or is there a Divine power behind our being? These questions intrigue me and were the reason I wanted to study theology formally.

Be open to the uncertain. Accept that you may not know what your path will look like. That is faith—walking into the unknown.

Draw on your courage to touch and transform other lives. It takes courage to decide to use a spiritual perspective to lead. It is contrary to the "acceptable norm" in business, but ultimately, you'll be a hero because your financial performance will explode.

It doesn't matter what you are doing, what your product is, or what your company does. You can lead this way if you move forward with philosophical insight, psychological maturity, and unconditional love.

By making a conscious decision to think big and play large—rather than shrink and play small—the true underlying potential of you and your people surges from vision to action to achievement. Let's discuss some examples of how to apply this principle to managerial applications.

## THE VISION

You have to think big to articulate a daring and exciting vision of the future for yourself, your team, your company, and its various stakeholders. I'm not talking about a "five-year strategic plan" that weighs about five pounds.

You've done the basic research on your market.

You then define where you're going with a focus on revenue growth. The quantum model demands that you at least double or triple your market growth.

You have a strategy that's focused on superior execution, particularly in your sales organization, market sector focus, distribution, and marketing support. That's ultimately your key differentiator, and it all revolves around the singular force of relationship selling.

In quantum terms, you want to realize a 20% to 25% operating margin and budget accordingly. The key to this is developing the right team and management process and, through a precise tactical game plan and meticulous execution, generating productivity rates an order of magnitude greater than your competition. (At Ascend, we were operating at three to five times the competition).

You can then project your financial model, market share, and market value based on the multiples in your industry. I used our projected market value to estimate for our people the potential value of the stock options they'd be granted IF we were able to perform at the quantum level, quite a powerful motivating process.

## QUANTUM GOAL SETTING

Quantum goal setting is another powerful example of how thinking big and playing large can be applied in the business world. Most companies do it all backwards. Lowball forecasts are the rule in what's called bottoms-up planning. People want to cover themselves, so they hold back. They don't want to put it all on the line. Budgeting and headcounts are set to meet a plan that is inherently self-limiting when done in the traditional manner.

By contrast, the leader focused on quantum performance studies the basic data about his industry including market segment, growth rates, market shares, competition, competitive productivity, and the company's product-positioning strategy. He's done all the right things to create a strong organization and develop a high-performance culture.

Then he demands the company grow at least two to three times the rate of the market and competition. He establishes the financial goals in a top-down process and only then asks what is needed to support the quantum goals to which he has committed the company. The true leader understands that what you demand of yourself and others is what you get. You take your people to a level of achievement they could have never envisioned. Ultimately, this perspective becomes the norm, and your company and people are positioned for actualization, the realization of true potential.

Understanding at a deep spiritual level the power and presence available to us all and not shrinking or playing small gives us the foundation to accomplish great things. Thinking big and playing large, even against giant competitors, was indispensable in giving us the confidence to achieve record-setting performance.

## Chapter Summary

- You were designed to be brilliant, gorgeous, talented, and powerful. When you look at yourself from this spiritual perspective, the world changes.

- The more we act a certain way—positive, negative, big, small—the more the behavior gets ingrained in our brain circuitry.

- Faith gives the license and energy to think big and play large. It requires leaping into the unknown.

- Not shrinking or playing small guides you into radical and transforming visions for yourself, your team, and your company.

- You think big, you play large, you set quantum goals—and then you just go for it.

# CHAPTER 3

## DARE TO LOVE AND
## THE NUMBERS WILL FOLLOW

*"The truth is that love is the ultimate and highest
goal to which man can aspire."*
*Viktor Frankl, Man's Search for Meaning*

Viktor Frankl's *Man's Search for Meaning* is the most profound book ever written. It exemplifies how powerful love is no matter what the circumstance. Frankl was a prominent psychiatrist in Vienna when he and his family were shipped to Auschwitz by the Nazis. He lost everyone in his family there and, to save his sanity, decided he would observe various behaviors among the prisoners. He writes about the power of love even in the hell he and others were locked into. Those who were able to reach into their hearts for love made the experience bearable for themselves and others and gave a deep meaning to their suffering. They were able to march into the ovens with their heads held high and a prayer in their hearts.

I saw Frankl interviewed on European television. He was 90 years old and, even with his horrible memories, projected an incredibly warm personality. He laughed frequently and had a great sense of humor. Amazing, and a wonderful testimony to the power of living a life based on love.

## A GLIMPSE OF CORPORATE LOVE

One of the companies I love is Southwest Airlines. I met the man who ran it for years, Herb Kelleher, in Dallas. What a character he was. He laughed and joked and told stories while chain-smoking unfiltered cigarettes and drinking Wild Turkey. He was one of the most magnetic individuals I've ever met and was a pure manifestation of love. He greeted every employee with a bear hug.

He had a simple game plan when he started Southwest.

Get passengers where they are going. On time. Set reasonable prices. *And* make their travel experience fun.

If you've ever been around a Southwest operation, you've see love in action. I remember boarding a Southwest plane in some kind of grumpy mood. I heard some mild chuckling up front and then it turned into real laughter.

When I raised my head to investigate, you can imagine my surprise when I saw a flight attendant dancing down the aisle kicking her legs in the air as she closed the overhead bins. I joined in with the rest of the passengers—and my funk had gone. I've seen a lot of other Southwest employees focus on delighting their customers and having a lot of fun with one another, doing "things you just don't do."

Don't you just love it?

And now Southwest is one of the largest airlines in America, flying more than 65 million passengers a year. The company has frequently ranked first on Fortune's list of best American companies to work for. Its market value is larger than United, American, and Continental airlines combined.

Ever talk to those Southwest employees? They'll say, "Man, I love this company, and I love Herb." They are really saying, "I love this company because this company loves me."

Their tremendous success was created by one man with a simple game plan who modeled love to all. This is the case with Herb Kelleher, Trammell Crow, and Sam Walton.

## LEADING WITH LOVE

Some people don't know how to love, particularly in a work environment. That's the lesson we are here to learn. The more you love, the higher the performance. Most people do not get this.

They were trained to listen to that old stuff and follow the direction of an old, tired senior management for whom people are commodities and you shouldn't be "soft" or "get too close." As I've mentioned several times, the contrarian is the one who wins big in business. The Spiritual Capitalist uses love as a platform and then rises to another place, taking her people with her.

I think what God cares about is how you demonstrate love in your personal and professional lives. The paradox is, if you really develop love for the others on your team and lead accordingly, the numbers can explode. If you start taking love into your professional world, it will start overflowing into your personal life. You will see every person, every interaction, and every relationship with the white aura of love. It will change your life.

How do you, as a leader, integrate love into your very being? This is when you have to step back and consciously decide to make business a spiritual experience *with the focus of love*. This is when you look at everyone with whom you work and recognize uniqueness and innate preciousness within each soul. This is when you accept that people will let you down, miss commitments, and act in an unreasonable and self-centered way—and you decide to love them anyway.

If you love your people, you are sensitive to their issues, problems, and needs. I realize how radical it is for me to say that you don't have to insist your people leave their problems at home, but I believe that. Those problems can dramatically affect their performance at work. Sense when something is wrong.

I once had a guy call me and say, "Mike, my wife is divorcing me. I'm going downhill fast." I said, "Okay, I'll be there tomorrow. We'll have dinner tomorrow night. Bring your wife." So we had dinner. I told his wife, "You have two beautiful children, and your husband loves you so much. What will it take to make this work? He doesn't want to lose you. Will it help if he takes the month off to be with you and work on it?" That's extreme. Most bosses won't go there. But, this guy had been working too hard, spending too much time on the job, and had forgotten how important his wife was to him.

He called me weeks later and said, "You know, I practice what you taught me every day." He told me that he and his wife are closer than they've ever been.

## SAY IT (THE L--- WORD)

Let's say you have an employee who has not made the objectives for the quarter. One boss will say, "Well, you S.O.B., if this happens again, I'm firing your ass." The spiritual capitalist approach would be, "Joe, you have a good track record. What's up with your not meeting your goals? Let's identify the issues, and put a plan together that will get you back on track. I love you, and I care for you and your family. I want you to be successful because we need your contribution." Obviously, these are two very different approaches. This may sound simplistic to you, but corporate America motivates from a place of fear, not love.

Whoa. Saying "I love you"? In the *office?* I'm not talking about running to your employee all lovesick in slow motion as you gush, "I love you!" This is not a romantic thing and obviously should not cross professional boundaries. It matters *how* you say the words. But realize that men can love other men. And, men and women can express their love to one another as brothers and sisters that is not sexual or sensual.

This is the kind of love that happens in athletic teams, it happens when two police officers work as partners for a decade, and it happens in business when you are teamed together with a collective goal and the pressure and responsibility to make it happen. The way it comes out is, "Jill, you know I love you and appreciate you but I know you can do more than $2 million this quarter." Or, "Joe, you're doing a great job, I'm incredibly proud of you—hell, I love you. I love how we are building this business together." If the love is there, why can't you say it?

My point is that we don't say it enough, and we should say it more. It makes people feel valued and it's a tremendous motivator. I've heard those who have worked for me say, "Hendren wants my team to do $50 million this quarter. That's a real stretch. But he's always shown me love and support, and I'm going to find a way to do it because I love the guy."

That's the kind of love I'm talking about. It is loyalty, commitment, teamwork, and looking out for one another, and it energizes us to accomplish some amazing things. The Spiritual Capitalist uses love—not money or other things—as his greatest motivator. And the big numbers just develop spontaneously, kind of like magic.

## TOUGH LOVE

Sometimes you have to use tough love. That means confronting the individual and the issues in a no-nonsense manner. The focus is on ensuring the success of the company and all of its employees.

Love gives you the license to say, "Bill, I know you're good, I know you have the capabilities to make this happen, but what is going on? I know you can do it, and you need to take an honest look at yourself and see why you aren't performing. If I didn't think you could do it, I'd fire you. So, cut the crap and do your job. Bill, do I believe in you more than you believe in yourself? You're not going to let your company down, your customers down, your teammates down and, most of all, yourself. Okay, now let's figure out what we need to do to get you back on track and performing at optimal levels. I don't want to have this conversation again." This approach inevitably stimulates the good employee to the path of real achievement.

## CONSTRUCTIVE CONFRONTATION

The spiritual capitalist seizes opportunities to grow people and performance. You can't do that when you are afraid of confronting problems in your people. It's not so much confrontation as it is communication. Be honest when performance needs to change. I realize confrontation can be awkward, but do it from a place of love and courage and it becomes constructive and oftentimes leads to breakthroughs in relationships and performance. Make the conscious decision to confront your fear by turning the fear of confrontation into an avenue of love.

The truth is, people are afraid of direct, honest communication because it makes them vulnerable. Embrace communication. Put it all on the line, share who you are, your confidences and your fears, your worries. Just put it all out there. It doesn't advertise your shortcomings, it advertises your humanity and facilitates others' responding to you and helping you. Once the love and trust are established, you have a powerful connection.

Your people don't have to doubt or second-guess or question or read between the lines in search of a hidden agenda. They know and trust you. They're free to perform.

The corporate world has operated on paranoia, insecurity, and fear for so long that people have come to expect the worst from their leaders. They wait for the bottom to fall out or for the knife in the back. They talk about things like the company line. They view management as "them" and coworkers as "us." The Spiritual Capitalist embraces the "we" in every endeavor, and it may take time for skeptics to believe that the goodness of this approach is genuine and permanent.

Ultimately, people can tell whether you are conning them or leading them. Some people might not trust you right away because of the bad experiences they have already had, but if you are consistent, honorable, and worthy, they will believe in you and follow your lead. It's not just what you say, it's who you are. You can't lead this way if it is not real or born out of your soul. You can choose this path but not for manipulative, short-term results. Travel this path until it becomes fundamental to your character. It's a spiritual commitment.

## STARTING TO LOVE AGAIN

Many of us have experienced the advantages of working for a positive, optimistic, and loving leader versus the agony of working for a sour, moody, and negative jerk. The good guy makes everything seem possible and the organization excels while the jerk ultimately fails and leaves damaged souls strewn all over his path. We're now seeing numerous studies that empirically confirm this reality. What could be clearer—except most business leaders don't get it.

They look at love as that mushy, touchy-feely thing that's definitely not masculine or macho, particularly in the workplace. And they miss the greatest opportunity of a lifetime truly to connect with their people, to transform countless lives, and to optimize corporate performance.

When there is no love, pettiness dominates. Politics, rules, policies, jealousy, insecurity, fear, and dishonesty run rampant. How would you like to operate in an environment like that? And yet, business "leaders" scratch their heads over poor performance—and then think of all the external excuses why their companies don't perform properly. Yet the answer is right there in front of them.

We were designed by love to love; it's really a natural human predisposition. Yet somewhere along our journey, we forgot how. How do you start again?

First, determine to see the Divinity within each human being. When you're about to do something to someone that your internal moral compass is warning you about, step back and look for the Holy in that individual. Drop down into your heart and let love be your guide. It will instantly change your perspective and help you come from a place of love.

I had a real breakthrough in the St. Louis story I shared with you earlier, when I took on an office that ranked last in the country and turned it into Honeywell's best performer. When I first met the people, I made the effort to see the Divinity in each of them. That was challenging because they were all full of blame, excuses, and insecurity. But I got there through a conscious effort of love. I then saw them as innocents who felt no hope. When that vision hit me, I had all the motivation I needed.

## YOU CAN CATCH FEELINGS FROM ONE ANOTHER

The love in your interactions with others becomes contagious. They see a model and want to emulate it. They see the light of love and its power.

The human heart naturally resonates with love and others on your team will begin evolving to that sacred place. The reward you get is knowing you have touched and transformed lives while stimulating a level of performance that provides powerful financial and intrinsic rewards. In essence, if you make others feel better about themselves, you feel better about yourself. It is so simple, but hardly anybody gets it.

When you get your people laughing, caring, and high-fiving each other, you feel the energy and excitement. But most managers try to hold onto their power because of fear and actually inhibit their employees. My employees loved me because I allowed them to transcend the mundane, restrictive, debilitating, boring, ugly facets of corporate life.

A leader liberates people, and people liberate their leader. I was liberated. My God, look at what we were accomplishing! It was awesome. I was making those outrageous predictions, and we were actually exceeding them! We performed brilliantly, all by eliminating their fear and energizing their love.

## FEAR VS. LOVE

I'm going to use the following chart to give you a road map to growth and freedom. We're talking here about the difference between fear-driven behavior and love-driven behavior.

| Fear | Love |
|---|---|
| Stay in the office | Get out with your people |
| Stick to the policy book | Do what you think is right |
| Don't get involved in their personal lives | Be there for them no matter what |
| Control their actions | Empower them to their potential |
| Hide your insecurities | Speak honestly when you need their help |
| Suck up to senior management | Make the team the priority |
| Micromanage actions | Embrace their efforts to grow |
| Don't get too close | Love your brothers and sisters |
| Intimidate with power | Liberate with love |
| Accept poor performance | Set them free |
| Make work drudgery | Offer opportunity for self-actualization |

## THE COMMITMENT

Try this little experiment. Commit yourself for a week to come from a place of love in all your business and personal dealings. Whether it is with your employees, your boss, your customers, or anyone else you encounter, in particular, your wife or husband and kids, you'll maintain constant focus on a platform of love no matter the nature of the interaction.

Try this for a week, and then ask yourself these questions:

1. How did you feel about yourself?

2. What did you see in others when you interacted with them on this basis?

3. Did you see a change in the spirit of your team?

4. Was it a good week for business?

5. When you put your head on your pillow at night and thought about the day, how did you feel?

6. When you woke up in the morning, were you more enthusiastic and excited about going to work?

7. Did you look forward to seeing the other people with whom you interact on a regular basis?

8. Did you change your opinion about some people?

9. Did your romantic life improve?

10. If you attended your church or place of worship, how did you feel?

Coming from a place of love will take you to another level. It's integral to achieving quantum sales performance and a new level in relationship selling. Let's discuss each.

## QUANTUM SALES PERFORMANCE

As the leader of an organization that was characterized at the time by analysts as the fastest-growing company in the history of American business, I'm often asked what the keys are to realizing such an accomplishment. I'll give you an overview of the actions I took in positioning us for the quantum financial performance we achieved. Understand the fundamental dynamic driving many of these actions was grounded in the type of love we've been discussing. New employees described our culture as a literal lovefest—and it was.

We knew the top line was the key—you can't save yourself to profitability. If you're achieving spectacular revenue growth, it seems that everything else just takes care of itself.

The key actions I would take in turnaround situations included:

1. Released sales managers with underperforming teams quickly in a caring and compassionate manner. You can't risk the welfare of the team because of a marginal manager.

2. Got close to the sales team so I could take appropriate action with marginal performers.

3. Armed myself with a compelling vision, powerful leadership presence, career growth opportunity, and highly leveraged compensation packages including equity. I then recruited competitive superstars who had a proven track record in our market and brought prospects and customers with them.

4. Used quantum goal setting as the norm.

5. Became the absolute best in relationship selling.

6. Targeted high-profile accounts that gave us credibility against our much larger competitors and worked closely with us in product development.

7. Created a lean, real-time management process that ran our business on a weekly basis when we were small and when we were $1 billion-plus.

8. Religiously practiced Spiritual Capitalism as our core business philosophy.

Salespeople need to be sold on what their job is. Sound somewhat paradoxical? Not really, because my definition of the great salesperson is:

- Achieves extreme quantum goals.

- Transcends and manages all problems.

- Is all about professionalism and integrity.

- Doesn't confuse effort with results.

The first thing I did was made sure that our salespeople made big money for making big numbers. When someone wants to go "cheap" on sales rep compensation packages, they'll get a marginal sales force at best and condemn their company to marginal results.

I supplemented their highly leveraged compensation plans with lucrative stock options for upside financial motivation and to develop a shareholder mentality. I used the question, "What would a shareholder want us to do?" to stop tangential discussion not in synch with our primary objectives.

Next, I emphasized and talked relentlessly about their sacred responsibility, to reinforce the huge part they played in supporting every employee's family.

Then I got into the real world with them. By that, I mean there were fundamental challenges in our industry and perfection was rare. I managed the sales force's expectations, repeating again and again that they should expect problems like product delays, poor product quality, poor marketing, poor support, etc.

I told them if the world were perfect, they sure as hell wouldn't get the pay packages, stock options, and other perks they received. It's not supposed to be easy—and that's what makes it fun. I drilled into our sales force the concept of "that's why they pay us the big bucks" to underscore our responsibility and accountability.

To emphasize the importance of their teams' achieving quantum performance on a consistent quarterly basis, my regional VPs knew if they missed a quarter, we would have a long talk to determine what went wrong and develop a tactical game plan for the next quarter with the required resources to get their area back on track. They also knew, given their responsibility for so many employees, that missing two quarters in a row was totally unacceptable and would cost them their job. A few missed a quarter every now and then. No one ever missed two quarters in a row.

My focus as head of sales was on managing the sales organization, not the sale. This is an important principle for all of you sales VPs. Because we were all great salespeople at one point and love the rush of closing deals, the temptation exists to insert yourself too frequently into sales campaigns. If you have the right team, there's no reason to do that except in rare situations. You get far more leverage focusing your time on leadership and management issues.

Our sales team always knew the quantum goals were coming. They might swallow hard, but given the rewards, riches, and responsibility available for achieving them, they committed themselves to ensuring they were realized.

I had a lot of fun with the sales teams during our quarterly reviews and used some of my favorite sayings. While the expressions were lighthearted, everyone got the point. When they started presenting mountains of data justifying their lowball forecasts, I assured them it was not necessary because their numbers for the quarter came "from a prescient dream I had received from above." When the excuses started to come for a missed month or quarter, my retort, "Excuse me, what's your mother's phone number? She might listen to this but not me." To those who insisted they just couldn't get to the quantum number I assigned, "I guess I believe in you more than you believe in yourself!" When someone told me how hard they worked, "Never confuse effort with results." Funny how these light but ultimately truthful responses served to end extraneous conversation. Try them with your sales team.

And at the end of the day, we all knew we had a critical job to do—take care of our employees, their families, our company, and our shareholders.

Here's one of my poems that you can share with that group of warriors you want to walk on water.

# Transcendence

You signed up for it
You enrolled yourself

Valor and courage
A willingness to take the heat

And like a warrior
You march into the streets
To do battle
For their hearts and minds

With your pin-striped armored suit
And wing-tipped feet
Ready to soar

To care for all the others who depend on you

With victory comes

Praise

Riches

Rewards

With defeat comes

Pain

Loss

Humiliation
But of course you know the rules

How the cards are dealt
The burden to carry
The pressures to endure

And despite it all

You transcend

You fly into the middle of the sun
You slay the fiercest dragon

You walk on water


## RELATIONSHIP SELLING

A lot of companies have competitive products in a good market. Typically, every market sector has a number of companies whose products will satisfy the customer's needs. Each competitor will have some marketing support, a distribution strategy, and a reasonably effective sales organization.

So what is the key differentiator? It's *relationship* selling. It's about developing a close and intimate relationship with your customer, one based on trust and mutual respect. It's creating a genuine professional and personal friendship where there's real caring and love for each other that transcends the issues and problems that inevitably arise. You know you're going to be there for each other, no matter what. You have some quality time away from the office where you really get to know each other, not only as a business associate but also as a person and friend.

You know the old axiom: People buy from people. If you were considering several companies as potential suppliers and all had products that could satisfy your requirements, but one had a sales rep that was able to develop a warm and genuine relationship with you, whom do you think you'd wind up doing business with?

It's really that simple and that profound.

Sales groups love to hear the following story, which gives you a sense of what relationship selling is about.

Some years ago, I received a call from our regional manager whose territory included Arkansas. If you had Arkansas as part of your territory, that meant only one thing—Wal-Mart. The problem was that our primary competitor, which was about a thousand times larger than us, considered Wal-Mart one of its blue-chip strategic accounts. So when he called to say we had a chance to get into Wal-Mart, I asked him if he had been smoking something funny. After a while, he convinced me to go to Bentonville, Arkansas, with him (not exactly on my Top 10 list of cities to visit) and discuss the possibility of a business relationship with Wal-Mart.

I met with the EVP of management information systems and told him while we were thrilled at the apparent opportunity to earn some business from them, he needed to know our size and that our sales campaign would strain our resources. Given the relationship with his current vendor, I wanted assurance that a decision would be based on an objective evaluation. In other words, please don't waste our time and resources unless you're ready to make a major commitment to a much smaller company at the expense of the surprise, wrath, or dismay of the incumbent with whom Wal-Mart had about a $75 million investment.

I got my assurance, so we decided we'd go for it. We knew our products could do the job. We had engineers at company headquarters on 24/7 to insure our products were optimized for

Wal-Mart. We had demo products and two engineers on site working directly with the technical staff in Arkansas.

When we began getting positive feedback from the Wal-Mart technical staff, we decided to bet the ranch on getting this $30 million deal and made the decision that we would not leave Arkansas until we got our order. We would be positioned to respond immediately to various issues, make a strong statement, and get to know a lot of Wal-Mart folks, supporters, buddies, inside skinny, etc.

When I told the EVP of our plan to stay in Arkansas, he had quite a chuckle. When he asked if I were serious, I told him, "Absolutely," and that he could look forward to seeing us in his lobby every morning until we got our order.

It was awesome. We were the talk of the company. We became party central for Wal-Mart employees each evening at our hotel. Then we would be there to greet everyone the next morning in the lobby.

Our last grand idea was to go "total Wal-Mart." What that meant was we put our Armani suits aside and started wearing an all Wal-Mart wardrobe as another kind of statement.

When our competitor finally got a sense of what was going on, its private plane brought several executives in to explain to Wal-Mart that it was foolish to entertain another relationship. That really irritated the folks in Arkansas, and that's when I knew we could get this deal. A few days later, while sitting in the lobby wearing our Wal-Mart shoes, pants, shirts, socks, ties, and underwear, we got the phone call from upstairs. To make a long story short, they're still talking about our celebration party in Bentonville.

## Chapter Summary

- Love is the ultimate goal to which man can aspire.

- The more you practice love in the business environment, the higher the performance. Most people do not get this.

- Love gives you a powerful license with your people. They accept and embrace forms of tough love directed at ensuring they realize their true potential. It is this dynamic that drives quantum performance.

- Constructive confrontation is an art that allows you to address and resolve issues immediately.

- The most significant competitive differentiator in building your customer base is in the power of relationship selling.

# CHAPTER 4

## EMBRACE LEADERSHIP AS
## A SACRED RESPONSIBILITY

*"There go the people. I must follow them for I am their leader." Gandhi*

In the previous chapter I shared a sales story with you about Wal-Mart and the power of relationship selling driven by a love for your customer. Wal-Mart had a unique and vigorous culture back then that fueled its incredible success. When you talked to employees, they described it in simple and powerful terms. Sam Walton embraced all his employees and customers as family and treated them accordingly. The employees in turn were totally committed to making his vision a reality. A current of love you could actually feel in the corporate office energized them to build the largest company in the world.

What did I really see in Wal-Mart back in those days?

- A leader, Sam Walton, with a simple vision and game plan all powered by love.

- True professionalism.

- Meticulous execution.

- A sense of humor and lightness.

- ROI that came with a loving dimension to its business relationships.

Sam Walton saw leadership as a sacred responsibility and embraced it with the power of love. When employees talked about him, their speech assumed an almost holy dimension. He was a father figure to them, and they knew that his model was a reference point for their behavior with one another and their customers.

You could feel the palpable energy of love permeating Wal-Mart. Think about it: A man from Bentonville, Arkansas, with a not-too-exciting business plan (I'm sure it was written on a napkin in some little restaurant) builds the largest company in the world. Now, what do you think was the key ingredient in this mammoth achievement?

Yes, you know, a strong spiritual love served as the foundation for the meticulous execution and energized the employees to work as a committed team to build this great company. Mr. Walton was one of the original Spiritual Capitalists.

## A SACRED RESPONSIBILITY

The people who work for you depend on you. Their families depend on you. Their futures depend on you. Their ability to reach their true potential depends on you. They have been placed in your hands. If you treat your responsibility as sacred, as did Sam Walton, you fuel your company with an immense force that carries it into a different sphere of achievement.

I know this principle of sacred responsibility has played a huge role in my success, and we've seen leaders of great companies like Herb Kelleher and Southwest Airlines, Trammell Crow and the Trammell Crow Company, Lou Gerstner and IBM, Richard Branson of Virgin, Brad Anderson of Best Buy, and Douglas Conant of Campbell Soup Company embrace its power.

## THE TRADITIONAL REGRESSIVE MODEL

Most businesses are overmanaged and underled because managers are insecure. They try to control employees versus empowering them. There is no trust. Fear pervades, and the only way some managers know how to put that fear in check is to try to overcontrol, overmanage, overdiscuss, overthink, overpower, and overplan—all to overcompensate for their fear and insecurity. They have no real understanding of the truth and power of love.

The traditional business culture is underled because the people in charge don't have the courage to empower the people who work for them. They don't understand that true leadership is plural, never singular. They think small, rather than big. They have no real vision of the true potential of their people and their company—and even of themselves.

## LEADERSHIP AND MANAGEMENT

There's a hunger for knowledge about leadership. It entails a limitless sense of what you have to offer and an unflinching commitment to the fulfillment of your destiny. It involves certainty in the face of uncertainty and skepticism and a magnetic quality in attracting and motivating followers.

Leadership and management are two different yet complementary disciplines. By-the-book management misses inspiration, vision, and the full spectrum of human drives and desires. Managers promote stability, while leaders press for change.

Companies manage complexity, first by planning and budgeting. Leading begins by setting a direction, a vision of the future, along with strategies for producing the changes needed to achieve that vision.

Leadership involves painting the vision and showing the way. Leadership is about believing in people more than they believe in themselves. Leadership is about taking your people into battle while exuding confidence that breakthrough levels of performance are possible. Leadership is about a depth of love for your people and your company that you can feel, you can touch, and you can live.

Management is about tactical game plans. It involves developing a process that monitors your progress toward your goals. Management is ensuring you have the right team members focusing on high payoff activities.

Leadership provides the vision and management insures the vision is realized. I've seen leaders who aren't good managers, and managers who aren't good leaders. Optimally, in terms of executive competency, the two disciplines are integrated seamlessly.

A great leader creates feelings of significance, community, and excitement. The sociological and psychological literature tells us that people seek, admire, and respect—that is, they follow— leaders who produce within them three emotional responses:

1.  A feeling of significance. They'll give their hearts and souls when they know they really matter. This comes from the human drive to be valued. Their lives have been given meaning.

2.  A feeling of community. With a unity of purpose, people are willing to relate strongly to one another.

3.  A feeling of excitement. A great leader creates a buzz among her followers. They want challenge and an edge in their lives that makes them feel engaged in the world.

When the leader defines a vision, she must motivate and inspire. The leader keeps people moving in the right direction, despite major obstacles to change, by appealing to untapped human needs, values, and emotions. Her people have to comprehend an alternate vision, one that can take them to an exquisite level of performance.

True leadership unleashes the organization's latent energy. Throughout this process the leader has the emotional capacity to embrace the uncertainty, frustration, and pain that's innate in transformation.

The leader generates a collective self-confidence throughout the organization while unlocking its people's creativity, passion, imagination, and willingness to take risks. The leader invests her time and soul in making the vision a reality by continually focusing on creativity and intuition and transcending the bureaucracy that can sink lesser men and women.

Many times, you must embrace chaos as the vehicle for change. Chaos reigns in business, and lesser leaders become engulfed in its tentacles. The Spiritual Capitalist expects the unexpected and, in fact, thrives on the upside opportunity it creates.

As a leader, you take your people from where they are to where they have never been. You shun the incremental; you go for it all.

You will know you're a true leader when your team consistently turns in quantum performance levels in a cultural environment rich in joy, passion, and love.

## PAINT YOUR VISION

As I mentioned in Chapter 2, think BIG. Hardly anyone does that anymore. The typical mind-set regarding vision, especially when you tie quantum projections to it, gets very conservative. It sounds like, "Whoa. It's time to cover my butt, I'm not going to stick my neck out. Maybe I can get lowball numbers through."

With this cowardice and lack of self-confidence, you'll never experience the greatness to which you are entitled. Rather, you visualize the ultimate, define the ultimate, and commit to quantum goal setting. The major benefit in doing this is that you articulate your vision in a way that inspires your people and your company to GO FOR IT!

Gulp hard with the numbers you decide on, look down from the twentieth floor, make sure your cape is on, and JUMP!

It's simple. You're a manager of a department, and you say, "If my department could perform at an optimal level, what would that look like? What would we have achieved? What would our culture look like? How would the people feel when they come to work every morning?"

From a corporate point of view, it is not just seeing what is possible; it's attaching numbers, timetables, and plans to your vision. Don't limit yourself by what you have seen or accomplished in the past. This is an activity focused on possibilities, and the past is the past. You are redefining the word "potential." Be creative, be bold, and be certain that anything is possible with a meaningful vision carried forward with the right leadership.

> ### Think Quantum
>
> *It is easy to set realistic goals and realize them. It is far harder to see all the possibility that exists, set what seem to be crazy goals, then reach and exceed them. People excel when they feel great, and the Spiritual Capitalist inspires that greatness. Your challenge is to look at your current circumstances and start thinking "crazy big." What could your company accomplish if your people were operating at twice their current level? Three times?*

Great leaders insist their people surpass themselves. They can see the individual's potential more than the individual can. The leader draws a vision for every individual of all the possibility that exists and, in so doing, inspires the person to achieve that level.

Breakthrough leadership cuts through old habits of thinking and adopts a fresh and innovative approach. You break through the limits imposed by your doubts and fears to achieve what others see as impossible.


## PEOPLE ARE SACRED

What do you want to do with your life? Do you want to touch and transform lives? Do you want to take your team to another level of performance that it could never have envisioned? Do you want to have joy in your workplace?

We've talked a lot about leadership as a sacred responsibility. If you want to transform yourself, others, and your company, then you need to go to a transcendent level of leadership. When you are given the responsibility for others, you have to lead. Leading, by definition, is taking responsibility for other people.

When I lead a team of people, I embrace the challenge of revenue growth as a sacred responsibility. Products

---

### The Purest Motivation

*The responsibility a leader carries for the spiritual well-being of her people can be utterly daunting. A cross word at the wrong time can be devastating to a human being who is in need of a pat on the back. Offhanded criticism may be remembered for years. Think about the "leaders" in your life—good and bad. What did they do to inspire you? In what ways did they turn your spirit on or off? Did they make you feel good about yourself, or bad? Which traits would you choose to emulate, and which would you use as examples of how you don't want to lead? You will constantly evolve in your role as a leader, but travel this path knowing that what you say and do will have great impact on the lives of the people around you. If you are driven only by the power or perks of leadership, you'll miss the pure human element that gives the most personal and lasting rewards of leading.*

can be developed, advertising can be done, marketing departments can market, but if a company does not grow and achieve aggressive sales goals, it risks current jobs, creating new jobs, and providing salary increases and promotions for employees. A lack of growth impedes the company's ability to provide a first-class work environment with the right productivity tools. The end result? Overworked employees, less family time, more lost jobs. Lost dignity for employees. Domestic problems, poor work environments, high pressure, stress and burnout, and, of course, corporate financial underperformance.

At Ascend, I frequently talked to our organization (more than 3,000 people across the world) about this sacred responsibility, and it was a strong factor in our success. I always ensured that when members of the sales organization were visiting our headquarters, they spent quality time with the people in the support departments. I personally liked to walk around the factory, where some of our poorer and less educated employees worked. You look them in the eyes and tell them you will make it happen—I'm talking about changing their lives—big time.

Factory workers, administrative people, service techs, and receptionists all fall under the philosophical perspective of sacred responsibility. And we did a good job of honoring the art of leadership and recognizing the tremendous impact on our people.

I'll say it again. The people who work for you depend on you. Their families depend on you. Their futures depend on you. So, you have literally the future and the well-being of multiple families in your hands. Look at each of those individuals and see not only the dependency that each has on you but also the spark of Divinity in him or her. The universe has placed your employees' well-being in the palm of your hand. It is truly a sacred responsibility, and you must treat it accordingly. If you do so, coming from a true place of love, you can take your team to a level of performance and fulfillment that you never dreamed possible.

## BELIEVE IN YOUR PEOPLE MORE THAN THEY BELIEVE IN THEMSELVES

You succeed by making others succeed. Your success is the aggregate of the performance of your team members. If you can make them peak performers, then your performance as their leader is obvious.

First, you must make sure they are capable of succeeding in their jobs in your company. That's all done by hiring slow and firing fast, disciplines we'll discuss later in this chapter. Then, once that person is fitted properly for her role in the company, you focus on believing in her and stretching the individual by painting the vision by which she can evolve. It's your vision, her vision, and the company's vision which all come together.

Sometimes people think that's too simple, but it *is* simple. It is the truth. At a certain level, you say, "Look, what I need from you is this. I need you to do $1 million this quarter. I can give you my ideas, but at the end of the day, make the $1 million." It's saying, "I know you can do it. Tell me what it takes to get there. I know you have the capability, talent, drive, and motivation. You might not think you can get there, but you can. Now, tell me what you need from me."

In the Orchot Tzaddikim, a book of ethical Jewish teachings from the fifteenth century, it is written, "The test of humility is your attitude toward subordinates." Your subordinates are *you*. If *they* underperform, *you* are underperforming. It's your job to lead them to achieve unparalleled results, and when they fall short, it's your job to talk to them and say, "What's going on here? What is the problem? What are the issues? What created these issues? What steps are we going to take to resolve the problems?"

Employees often feel humiliated by managers who may not even know their insensitivity is hindering performance. You have to become aware of this issue. You must ask in a deep and honest manner, "Why is my team not performing?" Or someone above you can ask the question. Or you can read a book to stimulate action on your part. The key is to define the main factors holding back excellent performance.

If you think insensitivity is an issue, get your people together and say, "I'm reading this book that talks about employers being insensitive. I need some feedback. I need to know if this applies to me. Are there issues I need to deal with that will help us achieve quantum performance?" Get your team together and collaborate on necessary actions.

Just being able to talk to your people openly will create an environment of performance rather than one where people are afraid to tell you the truth and focus only on telling you what you want to hear. Know what your people expect of you, and tell them what you expect of them.

I've seen companies use anonymous surveys to determine what the problems are. A company that is developing a high-performance environment does not need to do it anonymously. The people will feel free to say what needs to be said. You have to know the issues in order to solve the problems. Work toward open, honest, two-way communication that will help you to achieve the results you want. Then you will get to a point where the team moves forward as a team that demands more of itself than anyone else could.

## SHOW THEM THE WAY

Get your team together and collaborate on the support needed to achieve the quantum goal. It can involve people, products, and marketing support. Tell your people, "I don't want to limit us by what we've done in the past. I'm going to give each of you some goals that, when aggregated, will realize the vision I have painted." It is top-down leadership. I don't believe in bottom-up goal setting because people establish goals they know they can achieve.

You can't get to a quantum level of performance with those limitations.

This vision of yours isn't just something you are dreaming. You understand the market and the competency of your people. Your vision didn't fall out of the sky. It is bringing together a vision that involves the best possible performance and strategies of the people on your team.

You must directly confront any fear or insecurity that shows up in your team. You enlist your people in your vision by defining the logic, the rationale, and the rewards for achieving stretch goals. Everyone fears change, and some fear going to a level of performance that they never envisioned because people don't think big. They are insecure. They want to make sure that their goals are attainable versus stretching them to a new sphere of performance.

The specifics behind your vision of quantum level performance are that you understand your market's size and growth rate. You understand your product and how it is positioned competitively. Then you make the commitment to radical levels of performance. So it's: "Look, we're in a $10 billion market that is growing 20% a year. We are going to grow 50% by developing a great organization, creating a game plan that matches our vision, and carrying it out with meticulous execution."

How do you eliminate their fear? Again, the answer is so simple. Love. It's either love or fear. "Jane, you're the best there is. I'll back you 150%. I know you are going to give it everything you've got. I'll be there to help you see it happen." That's why you have to have the right people because they will make it happen. If you don't have the right people, you must fire the marginals because you cannot allow anyone to drag the team down. Once the right team is in place, you move it forward by being right there with your people, coaching them, cheering their success, and raising the bar for excellence.

## TAKING THEM TO A QUANTUM LEVEL

You've defined the aggressive goals, you've articulated a bold vision, you've liberated your people from the fears that hold them back, and the time has come to execute the plan.

Put a management process in place to monitor the team's progress against its stretch performance goal. In this way, you are constantly aware of where the team is, and any problems that arise can be addressed in real time. You look at the month-to-date performance on a weekly basis. If a team member is falling short, you discuss the reasons for the shortfall and the appropriate actions to ensure the monthly goals are achieved.

You stay on top of it. Every Monday, you talk. Here's your goal for the month, here's where you should be month to date. Here's where you are. Do you think you can meet your monthly goal? If you think you will have a shortfall, why? Is this an anomaly? Or is this a fundamental weakness in the team that must be addressed? If you are a player on the team, you know you are going to talk every Monday with your peers about whether you will meet your monthly goals. There is no place to hide. One team member is way ahead, and another is way behind. "What is happening? Come on, what kind of help do you need? You had a shortfall week one, you have a shortfall week two. Talk to me."

"Why didn't you?" should be a rarity in these conversations. Don't freak your people out with blame. They know you love them and believe in them. They know you are going to do whatever it takes to make them successful. There is a certain healthy tension in saying, "Yeah, you are paid a lot of money, you've got a lot of stock, and you've got to make this happen." But when they come in for the monthly meeting, they must know you are going to energize the whole company behind them to make them successful.

## DON'T KNOW EVERYTHING

An inflated ego is fatal to achieving outstanding performance. Most executives have inflated egos that create a barrier between them and their people and other employees. When the people on the team see a leader who is honest and forthcoming, they are immediately mobilized. For some reason, some executives are uncomfortable admitting their concerns and failures. This holding back of their truth affects the team's intimacy and performance.

The precipitating factor that makes some "leaders" reluctant to show their concerns is insecurity. You have to develop the courage to admit what you don't know. Admit your weaknesses. You may be a bit uncomfortable initially but the more forthcoming you are, the more comfortable you become. You see that discussing your weaknesses is a sign of strength. Ask them for their support. And identify a member of the team who can compensate for your weakness in a specific operational area.

The two most powerful statements you can make are, "I need your help" and "I'm sorry." The people who are afraid to use them are insecure because they think it shows weakness. But when you use those words, you are showing self-confidence and self-love. You say, "Hey, I've got a lot of great points, but this is one where I am not so sure. Can you help me out?" versus, "Let me hide in my office, I don't want my team to know I am weak and insecure in this area."

When others admit their failings, the team's intimacy of increases. In my case, we were generating incredible results, but I didn't have a deep knowledge of the technology we were selling. In fact, those wonderful members of my team loved to make serious fun of me in this area of extreme weakness. But I would go to Chicago, and my sales manager would be there with an engineer who had already presented the technology to the customer. I'd come in to underscore what relationship meant to us. Nothing substitutes for strong and powerful relationships with your customers or your people. So I added value to our effort by demonstrating to the prospects their significance to us. I would have added no value by pretending that I knew what I didn't know. That's why I had the right team to back me up.

Remember: Nothing is ever more important than being there for your people. I can never remember an instance when someone wanted ten minutes of my time and I couldn't give it to him or her almost immediately. My team members, not the board meeting, were the priority. I had the process we've discussed in which every Monday we had a teleconference for two hours talking about our business. If anyone needed to talk to me after the conference, we'd get right to it. Once a month, everyone would come in from the field for two days. If you have a process like that, it takes care of most of the problems that arise in real time.

## GO DEEP WITHIN

Leadership is a personal quest. While you strive to achieve the unthinkable, the challenge can sometimes plunge you into the dark as you search to grow into a true, enlightened leader. In simplistic terms, the leader looks at the performance of the team and analyzes problems if it is not achieving its goals.

Ask yourself a number of questions, like:

- Why am I failing as a leader?
- Have I defined the correct vision?
- Are we organized optimally?
- Have I hired the right people?
- Have I failed in motivating the team?
- Do I have confidence in my team?
- Do I have confidence in myself?

- Are our strategies effective?
- Is my management process effective?
- What is my gut feeling about what is going on?
- Do I have marginal players on my team?

Can you honestly and objectively ask yourself these questions? Do you know in your heart, soul, and intellect that you were meant to be a leader? You owe it to your people and yourself to have a rock solid belief in your leadership skills.

## CERTAINTY IN THE FACE OF UNCERTAINTY

The hallmark of a great leader is certainty in the face of uncertainty. Okay, how can you have certainty when things are twisting in a downward spiral? Project confidence. If the economy is tanking, the market is soft, and other companies are reporting record losses, how do you stay on track? If the market is down, it is down. Believe in yourself. Whether I was riding high waves or low waves, my people knew I was going to get them out of there alive. That's what your people need to know. They need to know what's going on.

Communicate with simple honesty. Get everybody together, get a bunch of ideas, throw them up on the wall, and see what sticks. "We can get through this, but we need your support and help. And, by the way, we are giving you an extra 1,000 shares of stock to get us through this." When all the news you see is bad, bring the gang together, admit there is a downturn, reexamine the dynamics of your marketplace, recheck your projected growth rates, and show leadership. Then you always paint the vision and show your people how all of you are going to get there.

## On Leadership

1. *Accept leadership as a sacred responsibility.*
2. *Make changing the status quo your priority. (See the steps below to change status quo.)*
3. *Define your quantum vision and how you're going to get there.*
4. *Learn to integrate leadership and management disciplines seamlessly.*
5. *Believe in your people more than they believe in themselves.*
6. *Build a collective self-confidence.*
7. *Learn the art of tough questioning, drawing out the issues, and managing conflict.*
8. *Use conflict as a source of creativity.*
9. *Develop the emotional capacity to handle uncertainty, frustration, and pain.*
10. *Brutally honest self-analysis allows you to be real.*
11. *Learn to say, "I'm sorry" and "I screwed up."*
12. *Strive for passion and excellence, not perfection.*
13. *Invest your time and your soul.*
14. *Leadership is not formulaic; trust your instinct, intuition, and your heart.*

Spiritual Capitalist principles guide your actions. If you choose love instead of fear, remember that love involves bringing your people in close. Fear keeps them away.

Love drives the actions that are commensurate with the principles of Spiritual Capitalism. If you believe that leadership is a sacred responsibility and incorporate that in your everyday acts in the workplace, your people will figure out what to do.

Troubled times affect your team in different ways. If you are the CEO, a middle manager, or a frontline employee, the impact will be different. No matter who you are, you'll see that downturns ultimately flush out the weak players. Don't be a weak player. Stay the course, and do your job to the best of your ability.

If you are a middle manager, analyze the situation and do all you can to practice the principles of spiritual capitalism. If you are a CEO and your company is not positioned well in a strong market, you reposition it . If your products or services are not competitive, you hire the people who can make them so. The company must be in a good market with good products. Then it's a matter of execution guided by Spiritual Capitalism.

The principles of Spiritual Capitalism work in good times and bad. When I first got to Ascend, we were a little company. We would go in for a sale, and our contacts would start liking us. But our competitors would tell them, "Why are you risking it on these little guys? They are nothing." So again and again, we'd hear, "I like you. I like your sales guy here. I've looked at your product, and it's competitive. But you've got 30 employees, and your competition has thousands. You're doing $12 million in revenue, and they're doing billions. I just can't afford to take the risk."

They'd feel that way because our competitor's sales guy was in that morning, saying, "You're going to take a winger on Ascend? But if they don't make it, guess who is going to lose his job? *You're* the idiot who made that decision. What do you think your CEO is going to say?" It took a lot to get beyond that.

Selling is all about relationships. So is Spiritual Capitalism. Getting skeptical buyers to bet on us meant we had to make a bond, a connection, with them. They had to believe in us. We had to stimulate their courage, their daring. And, yes, we made them feel loved, something none of our competitors seemed to think of.

These principles are the same when you are leading your own people and getting them to buy into your vision in tough times. Make the bond. They have to believe in you. You have to stimulate their courage.

Spiritual Capitalism brings out the best in people by mining their creativity and intuition without losing them to process and bureaucracy. It challenges their greatness and presents an avenue in which their greatness is manifested.

It worked within our ranks because advancing the company was a cause. It was transformative. You should have seen what it did for our people when we beat much, much larger competitors. There was a vision articulated and a way to get to there, no matter what obstacles appeared. And, as that happened, you knew the employees were saying, "Boy, do I love working for this company."

Let's discuss some managerial disciplines particularly important to the leader who understands her sacred responsibility and the impact she has on people's lives.

## HIRING

A powerful example of embracing leadership as a sacred responsibility is to hire slow and fire fast. The problem is that most companies do just the opposite, hiring quickly and terminating very slowly. When I tell companies they should fire fast, the typical response is it sounds like a harsh policy. In fact, it is based on love and respect for the individual, and you can do it in a compassionate manner, which we'll discuss, that's also cost effective and limits the possibility of being sued. On the front end, hiring is like a life-and-death decision for the individual, the company, and the manager.

Think of the impact on the potential employee and his family if your hiring decision is wrong. He's excited about his future, his family is proud of him, and he feels good about himself. If the hiring manager has not done a thorough job in making the decision, a destructive and hurtful chain of events will unfold.

We had an exceptional track record in hiring peak performers and, consequently, our turnover rate was practically nonexistent. Hiring slowly and in an intelligent and deliberate manner is critical.

Most managers don't do that. They're usually so excited about getting budget approval to hire that they rush out and get a body before the hiring budget is taken away. And they pay the price later. A wrong hiring decision is one of the worst management mistakes. It's damaging to the individual, the company, and the hiring manager. You must stress to your hiring manager that he has a sacred responsibility in this management discipline.

I always had the hiring manager, his boss, and myself in the interviewing and hiring process. The hiring manager was responsible for meticulously discussing the potential employee with former employers. We required W-2s to verify earnings history.

After several interviews, including discussions with the candidate's potential peers, I would meet with the prospective employee. Over time, I developed an intuitive feel for the type of person we wanted to hire—a peak performer, someone who could buy into our vision and culture and who would be delightful to have around. I could see it in their eyes and feel it in their hearts. You can cultivate this ability with focus and coming from a place of love.


## FIRING

I believe in firing quickly in a compassionate way. Of course, if you've done a meticulous and intelligent job in hiring, the occasions when you have to fire an employee will be minimal. The firing-fast principle makes most managers and HR departments shudder. They don't understand it and have a superficial perspective that produces lose-lose results.

Traditionally, the firing process goes like this. An employee is obviously marginal: He doesn't meet objectives, doesn't get the vision and culture, and isn't a lot of fun. The reason he isn't a lot of fun is that he knows he is in over his head. This is eating him up inside and crushing his self-confidence. But most hiring managers don't really care for their employees at a deep level and don't have the guts to confront the issue head-on. These managers keep kidding themselves that things will turn around, but they never do. So they delay making a decision for months.

Finally, they cop out and get the HR department to "handle" the problem. The first thing HR wants to do is develop a "performance plan" (I call it the Chinese torture test) for the next six to twelve months, which is a waste of time and money and humiliates the employee. I would bet that less than 5% of marginal employees turn around with a performance plan, yet managers and HR keep draining people and money with this ludicrous process.

Let me take a minute to make a brief comment regarding human resources, as I have been accused of giving these professionals a hard time. In fact, some of my best friends are in HR (a little humor here). Most HR people are just doing what they've been taught by the Traditional Regressive business model. It's worth your while to take some time to explain to these lovely people your philosophy and the day-to-day dynamics your team faces to ensure the company reaches a level of quantum performance. Focus the HR department on value-added services it can provide to support your efforts, such as a world-class fringe benefit program, information on what financial packages your competition offers, and finding transformative training classes that can help your people grow. Give these staffers stock options to motivate them to see the big picture.

Back to my approach to firing marginals. You have to have courage and genuinely care for the individual. When that first gut feeling comes and you know deep down he's not going to make it, have a caring and loving discussion with him to let him know he's in over his head. He already knows it deep down. Accept the responsibility you have in the situation.

Financially cover your marginal employee for a reasonable time frame while he looks for another job. This will typically cost you far less money than the Chinese torture test created by the HR department. The employee can resign honorably when he has a new position that is a better fit, avoiding embarrassment and family trauma. Typically, I would get a call from him in a few months thanking me for getting him out of a job he could not do and covering him financially during his transition. The person I fired had nothing but good things to say about our company. And the possibility of a lawsuit, which is very prevalent in today's business world, totally dissolved.

That is not only good business, it's an honorable and loving way to handle what can be a damaging and expensive process. Remember to invest a lot of time up front in the hiring decision. If you do have a marginal employee, act swiftly and decisively with love and compassion for the individual and his family.

## INTERVIEWING

Interviewing is critical in the hiring decision and in avoiding the destructive fallout from making a poor hiring decision. It should be an intuitive art, like reading their minds and hearts, directed by a structured approach to asking the right questions. We used a simple but powerful process to maintain an extremely low rate of attrition.

I insisted on asking the questions first and then gave the candidate the opportunity to ask me anything. When someone comes in and immediately starts asking lots of questions, my sense is that he is somewhat "scripted" and I would have an immediate concern.

The questions and comments I used to guide the process included:

1. "Tell me about yourself." This should be free-flowing. If they ask what you want to know, tell them it's about whatever they want to talk about. Here I want both

professional and personal information (marital status, children, childhood, parents, high school, college, avocations, and strong personal values and interests).

2.  "Why are you considering a change?"

3.  "How did you get here to talk with me?"

4.  "What are your professional and financial goals for the next year, and where do you want to be professionally three years from now?"

5.  "What are your three major strengths?"

6.  "What are three areas in which you can improve?" Force them to come up with this and no BS.

7.  "If I ask you to show me your W-2s for the past three years, what would they reflect?" (Some people will fudge these numbers without this approach.)

8.  "If I called your last two supervisors, what would they say about you? What were their major concerns regarding your performance?"

9.  "Tell me about your two most significant accomplishments with your current employer over the past twelve months."

10. "How much revenue can you produce for us in the next twelve months?"

11. "What prospects and customers can you bring with you?"

12. "What haven't you told me that I should know before I consider offering you a position?" This is your last chance to avoid surprises later.

The answers to these questions will tell you a lot. Then the quality and sophistication of the candidate's queries will tell you the rest. Take notes and share your impressions with others who have interviewed the person. Ideally, someone on your team is a former coworker and can provide invaluable input. Think through everything you've discovered. Talk to the others in the interviewing process. Take your time and you'll come to the right decision.

By embracing her sacred responsibility, the great leader generates a collective self-confidence throughout the organization by unlocking people's creativity, passion, imagination, and willingness to take risks. She transcends the bureaucracy that can sink lesser men and women. She has the emotional capacity to embrace the frustration and pain that can be a part of transformation.

Her artistry, heart, and inspiration emancipate the people and lead them on a journey into the world of quantum performance and self-actualization.

## Chapter Summary

- Most businesses are overmanaged and underled because managers are insecure. They try to control employees versus empowering them.

- Leadership is about believing in people more than they believe in themselves.

- You must make the conscious decision to work through the critical steps of transformation if you're genuinely committed to achieving quantum performance.

- Your sacred obligation as a leader is to take yourself, your team, and your company to the state of self-actualization.

- Managerial disciplines such as hiring and firing can be performed in a caring and compassionate manner that is far more effective than traditional approaches.

- The people who work for you depend on you. Their families depend on you. Their futures depend on you. They are your sacred responsibility.

# CHAPTER 5

# DEVELOP MANAGEMENT
# INTO AN ART

*"Shoot for the moon. Even if you miss you will land among the stars."*

*Les Brown*

The goal in developing management into an art is to liberate—rather than inhibit—your people's potential by creating an invigorating, high-performance culture.

The philosophical difference between the traditional and the Spiritual Capitalist approach to management can be illustrated by contrasting their inherent characteristics

As mentioned in the introduction, the original idea for this book was from a number of people who suggested I write about my business philosophy. I reviewed a range of business books and found most were written by academicians, consultants, and a few Fortune 100 CEOs. They seemed to have little real-world value for the typical businessman struggling with his everyday challenges. To address this concern, my focus in this chapter is to provide a mini how-to manual that will guide you in applying the Spiritual Capitalist managerial perspective.

We'll consolidate key points regarding all the examples of the Spiritual Capitalist methodology we discuss in detail throughout the book, so you'll have one place to go as a guide to managerial practices. We'll touch on:

1. The Culture
2. The Spiritual Capitalist Approach
3. The Vision
4. Positioning for Quantum Performance
5. Strategic Business Plans
6. Quantum Goal Setting
7. Quantum Sales Performance
8. Relationship Selling
9. Creating the Right Team: Hiring
10. Interviewing
11. Compensation
12. Creating the Right Team: Firing
13. Psychological, Financial, and Operational Ownership
14. Focus
15. MBO
16. Management Process
17. Performance Reviews
18. Don't Accept the Unacceptable
19. E-mail
20. Managing Expenses

## THE CULTURE

It all starts with building a high-performance culture that's stimulating and supportive while also being demanding and challenging. Lou Gerstner engineered a historic turnaround at IBM after previously serving as chairman and CEO of RJR Nabisco and president of American Express. He had no real experience in technology but was known as a tough and effective CEO.

His core competencies were strategy, analysis, and measurement. Sounds like a fun guy. But what he saw at IBM during his early days really got his attention. Instead of articulating some bold new strategy up front, he first had to address employee issues that were poisoning the work climate. He did things like change a stingy stock option program, eliminate the ban on drinking at corporate gatherings, abolish the regimented dress code, and, most important, work on getting IBMers to believe in themselves again.

Later, after a successful turnaround, he was frequently asked the most important factor in his success. It wasn't strategy, analysis, or measurement. "Culture isn't just one aspect of the game, it is the game," he said. He discovered that a strong and compelling culture is fundamental to transformation.

The high-performance culture defined in Chapter 1 is characterized by a compelling vision, quantum versus linear thinking, true ownership and empowerment, a powerful emotional energy, and the transformative power of love.

## THE SPIRITUAL CAPITALIST APPROACH

The Spiritual Capitalist manages with his head and leads with his heart, utilizing the intellect of the mind with the transformative power of love. I think exceptional senior executives possess a 60% to 40% mix of leadership and managerial excellence. After he has redefined the company's culture, he asks the thought-provoking questions articulated in Chapter 1, which challenge traditional thinking and lead to breakthrough approaches to managerial practices.

We've talked about leadership, management, and the need to integrate these two disciplines seamlessly in order to optimize performance. Let's look at what I consider the Top Ten responsibilities of each discipline and their complementary nature:

| LEADERSHIP | MANAGEMENT |
|---|---|
| Embraces Sacred Responsibility | Focuses on Individual Growth |
| Facilitates Transformation | Manages Complexity |
| Positions Company for Success | Implements Product and Marketing Strategy |
| Articulates Strategic Direction | Defines Tactical Game Plan |
| Creates High-Performance Culture | Utilizes Liberating Managerial Practices |
| Articulates Quantum Vision | Implements Company Direction |
| Demands Quantum Goal Setting | Establishes Stretch Performance Objectives |
| Promotes Collective Self-Confidence | Instills Empowerment and Ownership |
| Demonstrates Emotional Strength and Intelligence | Handles Change and Chaos |
| Actualizes Company | Actualizes Individuals |

## THE VISION

The type of vision referred to in Chapter 2 focuses on quantum performance and defines a bold future for yourself, your team, your company, and its shareholders. You concentrate on superior execution and project the financial model to which everyone is committed and the rewards it provides to all of your stakeholders.

## POSITIONING FOR QUANTUM PERFORMANCE

If you're in a good market and have a competitive product, your company can achieve a level of performance that you never dreamed possible. If you meet these two requirements, the issues regarding company, market, and product positioning have been addressed. Given these two fundamentals, the key variables leading to quantum performance are superb leadership and management execution. That's it.

## STRATEGIC BUSINESS PLANS

Instead of creating a lengthy and boring strategic plan that puts everyone to sleep, you create a precise twelve-month tactical game plan (discussed in Chapter 8) that defines the quantum financial model, individual responsibilities and time frames, and elements of the high-performance environment to which your company is committed.

## QUANTUM GOAL SETTING

As we discussed in Chapter 2, quantum performance requires quantum goal setting. The objectives are produced from a market-researched, top-down perspective focused on stretch performance versus the traditional bottom-up process with all its innate limitations.

## QUANTUM SALES PERFORMANCE

We discussed quantum sales performance in detail in Chapter 3. We created what at the time was the fastest-growing company in the history of American business by concentrating on the following:

- No tolerance for marginal performers.

- A compelling vision and highly leveraged compensation plan with upside earnings and stock options to recruit competitive superstars.

- Total focus on quantum goal setting and stretch performance.

- Being the best at relationship selling.

Our high-performance culture demanded the maximum effort from everyone.

## RELATIONSHIP SELLING

There will always be a number of companies in your market with competitive products. Your ultimate differentiator is relationship selling. You must develop a close relationship with your prospect and customer based on a genuine professional and personal friendship, which reflects a love for each other that transcends the issues and problems that inevitably arise. That old axiom that people buy from people is the bottom line.

## CREATING THE RIGHT TEAM: HIRING

The key managerial principle in building the right team is to hire slow and fire fast. On the front end, hiring is like a life-and-death decision for the individual, the company, and the manager.

Unfortunately, most companies have it backward. Instead of a deliberate and structured process for hiring, the manager hurriedly hires a body before his budgeted headcount is taken away. This is one of the key reasons for high attrition rates.

We talked in detail about this in Chapter 4.

## INTERVIEWING

Interviewing is an art based on a structured approach to asking the right questions. Done properly, it greatly reduces one of the worst managerial mistakes, a hiring error. We defined the process that we used with great success in Chapter 3.

## COMPENSATION

Compensation, which we address in Chapter 6 on empowerment and ownership, should be about quantum performance. You want to provide strong upside incentives for reaching exceptional performance. Stock options based on company performance are the ultimate avenue for the individual to enhance his material quality of life dramatically.

## CREATING THE RIGHT TEAM: FIRING

Fire quickly in the compassionate and caring way we described in Chapter 3. It is literally an act of love and far more cost effective than the traditional approach.

Instead of an angry ex-employee who says nothing but negative things about your company and contemplates suing you, you have someone who has great respect for you and the company.

## PSYCHOLOGICAL, FINANCIAL, AND OPERATIONAL OWNERSHIP

Making a genuine investment in eliciting your people's psychological, financial, and operational ownership of the company will provide you with a dramatic ROI. Chapter 6 illustrates the difference between the Traditional Regressive and the Spiritual Capitalist approach through managerial practices such as compensation, performance reviews, management process, and managing company expenses.

## FOCUS

I don't think most managers understand the significance of this discipline. The ultimate management guru, Peter Drucker, believed focus was the single most important management tool. In simple terms, you should write down each Monday morning what your top five objectives are for the week. They should be carefully thought out in concert with your major operational goals.

Then the rule becomes "If what I am about to do does not assist me in achieving my Top 5 for the week, then I am not going there." Despite all the various demands on your time, you must understand that focus is your most important resource.

You have to manage it intelligently and deliberately. In particular, learn to say NO to requests that do not address your Top 5. After you do this a few times, you'll feel its empowering effect. By precisely managing your time, you focus on the highest ROI activity available, the expression of your love and care for those for whom you are responsible.

My Top 5 usually looked something like this:

1. Make the numbers with a weekly focus on month-to-date consistency and balanced performance from my seven VPs.

2. Provide maximum responsiveness from myself and all company departments to our field operation.

3. Ensure world-class quality in our people throughout the organization.

4. Offer the highest possible level of customer satisfaction with an emphasis on finding creative ways of delighting those who place their trust in us.

5. Create and maintain a high-performance culture.

If you use this simple approach to focus, you'll improve your productivity dramatically.

## MBO

Management by Objectives can be a simple and powerful tool to facilitate the type of focus we've just discussed. If you or HR turns MBO into a paper-heavy bureaucratic process, then its potential is crippled. The power as usual is in simplicity.

When I talked with you about focus, I discussed my Top 5. I used MBO to define goals for my direct reports.

My regional VPs knew the fundamental requirement was to achieve our quantum financial goals, particularly revenue growth, while maintaining a 25% operating margin. This was always the primary quantitative objective.

At the beginning of each quarter, I would add five key qualitative objectives; they typically included:

1.  Balanced performance throughout their organization

    (not just a few superstars).

2.  Zero tolerance for attrition.

3.  New account penetration (don't just live off the customer base).

4.  Consistent financial performance (weekly, monthly, quarterly).

5.  True value-added input to optimize our tactical game plan.

The idea is to have a single piece of paper, signed by you and your direct report, which can be referred to at the end of the quarter for an objective evaluation of performance. Appreciate the honor involved in your joint commitment to the agreement.

## MANAGEMENT PROCESS

My guiding principle when it comes to the management process is the simpler, the better. The basic rule is that your people respect what you inspect. Managers should monitor performance and issues on a real-time basis while empowering their teams and honoring the principle of ownership. Chapter 6 gives a detailed explanation of the process we used, which helped us reach a level of extraordinary achievement.

## PERFORMANCE REVIEWS

Performance reviews are a waste of time, and everyone hates the whole process. If a manager is doing his job and is close to his people, the last thing he and the employees need is to endure this ineffective and time-consuming exercise.

If you have to do them, just give them to the employees and let them handle it. They're usually tougher on themselves than you would be, and it adds some fun and liberation to the whole futile process. We'll talk more about this in Chapter 6.

## DON'T ACCEPT THE UNACCEPTABLE

Don't accept the unacceptable. Sounds reasonable except most managers do because they're uncomfortable with honest and direct communication. Rationalizing away poor performance is crippling to the employee, the company, and the manager.

Have the heart and courage to speak frankly if your employee can't live up to the demands of a high-performance culture.

Constructive confrontation is the art we use in not accepting the unacceptable. Coming from a place of love for the employee, we demand that he live up to his potential or release him so that he can pursue another path.

## E-MAIL

Instead of accepting the norm of e-mail addiction, we use more intimate communications to lead our people. Wasted hours, misunderstanding, impersonal CYA messages, and unhealthy and draining obsession with e-mail have no place in the high-performance environment. I'll go into great detail about this subject in the appropriately named Chapter 7, Don't Take It All So Seriously.

## MANAGING EXPENSES

You can't let the bean counters focus on nominal incidental costs, inflicting brain damage on everyone. The real costs are the personnel ones: headcount, compensation, and benefits. Concentrate on headcount and productivity. That's the focus for optimizing profitability. A bit more on this in Chapter 6.

## Chapter Summary

- Management can be converted from an onerous constraint into a liberating art of grace and efficacy.

- It all starts with building a high-performance culture.

- The Spiritual Capitalist asks questions that intentionally challenge the Traditional Regressive model.

- Contrarian approaches to traditional managerial applications create greater results.

- A mini how-to manual gives you the flavor of a philosophy that took others and me to the pinnacle of professional and financial achievement.

I'll leave you with one of my poems that looks at the heart and soul of management.

# Management

Some say it's all about

Policies
Rules
Regulations
Politics

That road will kill the soul

It's really about

Heart
Spirit
Kindness
And Compassion

An art

Of grace and elegance

Embraced with the courage
To love and care for people
And take them on a path they never dreamt

To transform

Lives
Families

Companies
Each other

By choosing the road less traveled
The one straight to the heart

A spiritual experience
Full of God's challenges
And grace

A transcendent adventure
Into the realm of magic and miracles

Now the stage is set
And the actors await

You

Their leader
Friend
And lover

Which road will you take these precious ones on?

# CHAPTER 6

## EMPOWER THEM WITH OWNERSHIP

*"Life's most persistent and urgent question is*
*"What are you doing for others?"*
Dr. Martin Luther King

David Packard, one of the founders of Hewlett-Packard, said that we have a responsibility to our employees to recognize their dignity as human beings. He believed those who help create the wealth have a moral right to share in that wealth. He shared equity and profits with all employees, a radical idea thirty-five years ago. It's still a radical idea to most traditional regressive companies.

Unfortunately, most companies load up their senior executives with tons of stock options and basically ignore or provide only a token amount to their employees. Their greed blinds them to the incredible power behind making all employees shareholders. We've recently seen where this path of self-interest leads. If they had any sense, they would take a portion of their options and spread them out among the team members. What they had left would be worth even more to them because of the financial incentive and validation given to their employees.

The financial investment in equity participation makes a strong and tangible statement to the employee no matter if it's a middle manager, factory worker, or secretary. I saw the smiles on our employees' faces and the commitment in their hearts to do their part in ensuring the success of my last three companies, all of which practiced this policy.

You want to complement the financial statement you've made with the psychological empowerment that operational ownership provides. "Ownership" and "empowerment" are two greatly overused words in terms of managers actually putting them into practice.

Many times, the manager, trapped in a regressive and nonsupportive culture, becomes a control freak in a fruitless effort to counter his fear and insecurity. "Micromanagement" is the term we give this, and it not only diminishes performance but also kills the spirit.

---

### How Well It Works

*The argument for empowering with ownership is especially clear in a 2005 Journal of Business Venturing report. Business professors contrasted 50 rapid-growth companies with 50 slow-growth companies in the Orlando area and showed the results of such empowerment.*

*The rapid-growth companies had at least a three-year compound annual sales growth rate of 80% or more. Almost universally, these companies emphasized training, development, financial incentives, and stock options. Company leaders made growth a priority and maximized human capital to achieve their visions, reported business professors Bruce Barringer, Foard Jones, and Donald Neubaum.*

*To attract, motivate, retain, and get the most from their employees, these CEOs used performance-based incentives, like bonuses and profit sharing. Stock options and ownership were critical in these strategies. Because the employees had a significant financial stake in the success of the company, they drove the rapid growth. Once empowered with ownership and financial reward, the employees performed at levels inconceivable by competitors.*

---

## TRADITIONAL VS. SPIRITUAL CAPITALISM

Let's take a look at the contrast between the Traditional Regressive and Spiritual Capitalist regarding empowerment:

| TRADITIONAL REGRESSIVE | SPIRITUAL CAPITALIST |
|---|---|
| Equity to a select few | Stock options for everyone |
| Control, control | True empowerment |
| Control, control | Leadership culture |
| Micromanagement | Ownership and freedom |
| No variable income | Incentives for quantum performance |
| Looks at every little expense | Counts people, not pencils |
| Thinks small | Thinks big |
| Myopic | Visionary |
| Hounds | Liberates |
| Insecurity | Collective self-confidence |

If the leader is a Spiritual Capitalist, he has created the type of stimulating environment we've been discussing. He's ensured the company is positioned strategically from a market and product standpoint and created the right team to make the vision a reality.

So no one needs to be insecure or fearful, just come from a place of strong, demanding, and challenging love. The manager gives his people their goals, the appropriate support, and a salary, bonus, and equity package geared to quantum performance. He looks them in the eye, lets them know how much he believes in them, and then GETS OUT OF THEIR WAY!

Put yourself in the shoes of a secretary or a low-level factory worker. They struggle to make ends meet and, let's face it, they don't have the most fulfilling jobs in the world. What can you, an inspired leader, do to maximize their contributions (because you need everyone optimized to become a world-class company with optimal levels of performance)? You make them feel important because they are. You redesign their jobs with them to provide as much satisfaction as possible. AND you look them in the eye and into their heart —and congratulate them on becoming stockholders! Then the magic begins.

## SHOW THEM THE MONEY

It's really simple. Find out what salaries your competition is paying and increase those offerings by 20%. If you are leading a company to quantum performance, you have the financial power to offer more than your competition. And you sometimes have to do that to attract and keep the highest-caliber employees on your team. You want to target and hire the top people away from your competitors. If you want to be the key player, you have to play like it. Salaries make statements. They indicate the value the company has for its people. They show appreciation and reward.

But the real upside in compensation comes in its variable component. You want people to be rewarded commensurate with their goal achievement. My philosophy was always that salary paid the bills, and that variable compensation based on goal achievement represented the real incentive.

For example: "David, we've agreed on these three goals, you have your salary and I know, with the right level of support, you're going to make your base goals. If you achieve this higher level of quantum performance, you'll get another $10,000 on top of your salary this quarter. If you do twice as much, you'll get an additional $20,000." David is going to work like hell to get that extra $20,000. And—since his company awarded him stock options—as a stockholder, he's now additionally motivated to optimize his contribution. This type of compensation coupled with visionary leadership is what propels quantum performance.

## TRUE OWNERSHIP

As I mentioned earlier, if you look at the majority of companies, stock is provided only to the upper level. The concept of distributing equity to *all* employees is foreign. Maybe they should read about Hewlett-Packard, one of the most respected companies in the world. If it's good enough for HP, it sure is good enough for me. But because of their ignorance, they lose one of the most powerful sources of motivation in the business world.

So, what are we really talking about? We are talking about giving every single employee the ability to share financially in the company's success. Hello! What is so difficult about grasping this fundamental principle? What if your secretary had stock in the company? What if the guy on your assembly line had shares in the company? What if the engineer working on a new product had shares in your company? I could go on and on.

The major difference between providing stock options and letting your employees buy discounted stock is value. Options provide the real upside, and that's why senior management is loaded down with them. Many senior managers are so greedy that the idea of sharing the options with lower-level employees is a radical concept. They can raise hell about their people's performance, while denying them participation in the company's stock option program. They don't love their people enough to provide the financial freedom and security they want for themselves. Why does the corporate hierarchy create haves and have-nots, when all humans are motivated by the same desire for freedom and security?

Every person at our company had those financial incentives. The immigrant on the assembly line, the office clerks, even the janitors could achieve the opportunity for financial freedom for the first time in their lives. So let me ask you a question. Do you think they were motivated to do the best they could possibly do? Do you think they felt loyal to the company and wanted to stay and help it grow? Do you think they felt loved?

## THE OTHER KIND OF OWNERSHIP

Once the financial ownership is established, psychological ownership needs to be addressed. That means, No. 1, you hire the right people. No. 2, you provide them the support and resources necessary to achieve optimal results. No. 3, you paint them the vision of where they and the company can go.

So many times the insecure manager, lacking love and appreciation for the subordinate, is driven to micromanage performance. Instead of liberating the employee to achieve his or her true potential, that manager ensures through micromanaging that the true potential is, in fact, never realized.

Do you want to be a leader or a micromanager? Do you want to take your people to the pinnacle of success or bury them under report requirements? Do you want to look into their eyes and hearts or hide in your office behind the bureaucracy you have created? Is your vision inhibited by a myopic perspective on business and on life? The answer is to liberate your employees by providing them the ownership of their success. Take them on the voyage of self-discovery.

Financial is financial. It's an obvious investment with an obvious return. The higher payoff is through embracing the employees with love and confidence and allowing them to determine their destinies, to see how really great they are. They're led to develop a relationship with you, the company, and themselves that takes them to a higher place.

Once the power of love appears in the equation, world-class performance is possible. True ownership involves more than money; it involves soul. And this dynamic inspires individuals to reach their true potential.

Embracing them into your management team makes your people feel like they belong. You do this by including them in key meetings and asking them for input on operational issues. You collaborate with them. You let them do their own performance reviews. And, more than anything, you believe in them and tell them of your very genuine love for them.

This builds a psychological bond that empowers you to reach another sphere of performance and fulfillment. They know they matter, not just as producers but also as valued thinkers. Their opinions are actually heard. Their contribution matters on every level. There is no "us" and "them," but "we" and "we are all in it together." Not only do they have ownership in the company, they have ownership in its collective destiny.

## EVERYONE A LEADER

Develop a mind-set within each of your employees that he or she is a leader. Whether leading a department of people, an operational area, or as an individual contributor, everyone can be committed to performing at the highest levels. The empowering process naturally positions each employee for this path. No longer is it "just a job" to them, and no longer is corporate BS tolerated, and no longer do fear and insecurity rule.

You reinforce the financial and psychological equity in every interaction you have with your employees, underscoring ownership, accountability, and responsibility every step of the way.

You do things like:

- Ask them questions. (How radical!)

- Listen to their answers. (How radical!)
- Recognize their contribution and take them and their peers out to lunch to underscore the recognition.
- Take them and their significant others out to dinner.
- Handwrite notes thanking them for their efforts.
- Surprise them with an unexpected day off.
- Ensure their compensation is designed for quantum performance.
- Let them sit in on important meetings as representatives of their departments.
- Have your company president personally thank them for their contributions.
- TELL THEM YOU LOVE THEM for their work, their contributions, being team leaders, and just being their beautiful selves with all the wonderful qualities they bring to the company.

Now, I think you're going to have a very loyal, committed employee working at an optimal mode. What do you think?

Once you've empowered the employee with every appropriate type of ownership incentive, you then define what ownership means in terms of expectations you have of them.

This type of motivation and inspiration energizes people by satisfying the basic human needs for achievement, sense of belonging, recognition, self-esteem, feeling of control over one's life, and the ability to live up to one's ideals.

## THEY OWN THE VISION

Once you paint the vision, it is theirs to embrace. Intuitively, they will know it is their path to transcending the past with all its limitations. They are inspired by the confidence of the leader and believe in her ability to take them there. You can have the greatest vision in the world, but if the troops aren't marching with you, it dies.

You show them where to go, and you clear the path for them. You do what you can to minimize obstacles such as bureaucracy, politics, and resource limitations. It's your job to keep them focused and inspired.

Once they feel the ownership of the process and the vision, Spiritual Capitalism magic occurs. They are invested in their success personally, professionally, and financially. As they achieve their human potential, they evolve spiritually. And, when you've built a true team, a spiritual resonance permeates the entire organization.

You dream the vision, but they own it by giving it life.

## CUSTOMERS ARE MEMBERS OF THE TEAM

Start to see your customers as members of the team and emphasize their ownership in your mutual success. Even they can benefit from stock opportunities. You want them to own your success. You want them to participate in product planning. You want them to tell you what is right and wrong about your company. You want them to tell you what is right and wrong with you. As simple as it sounds, listening to your customers and engaging them in your success is not practiced as much as it should be.

It builds loyalty. They don't want to leave you because you love them and they love you. They can't look you in the eye and say, "We're going to a competitor."

When you realize that you have a reciprocal and loving relationship with your customer, you realize the power of intimate relationships. When I say an intimate relationship, I mean communication, honesty, integrity, and love. This type of customer relationship takes them—and you—to another level.

Give them support, the right products, and the right service and truly listen to and care about them. View your relationship with them as a strategic partnership, exactly as you should with your employees. Focus not on just meeting your customer's needs. DELIGHT them in every area of the relationship through the extra efforts inspired by Spiritual Capitalism instead of relying on the feeble minimalist approaches of the past.

When competitors attack, problems arise, and chaos reigns, the strategic partnership with your customer is an impenetrable fortress against competitive penetration.

## KEEP BELIEVING IN THEM MORE THAN THEY BELIEVE IN THEMSELVES

Understand and recognize that the majority of people initially will have trouble understanding the dynamics involved in quantum performance. They bring a weight of education and experience that is diametrically opposed to the truth of individual and team potential. This weight is self-regulating, self-imposing, and self-limiting. It needs to be released.

A leader practicing the principles we have been discussing can mitigate the damage done and unleash the people's true ability. The truth is a place where the shackles are broken and dreams come to life. Psychological and financial ownership enhance the commitment to the team's aspirations. It cements a bond that is transcendent in nature. Bestowing ownership proves that you believe in your people and their mission.

A leader communicates the vision and values of an organization. You must take every opportunity to reinforce the organization's vision and values constantly. Psychological and financial ownership is the most powerful tool to accomplish this.

Understand that we all come hardwired with the desire to contribute. A great leader complements this with the ability to offer people external and intrinsic rewards that provide the tremendous lift that comes from becoming aware of one's own talents and maximizing them.

There is also a spiritual component to this subject. Our life here on earth, this spiritual adventure, provides us many opportunities for growth. Our ability to meet the fear created by an opportunity determines if, in fact, it becomes an instructive growth experience.

## FLY ABOVE

By now, you know I'm a devout believer in quantum performance goals. And as you've read earlier, one of the biggest mistakes that businesses make is setting goals too low, not thinking BIG enough. Because of the confidence I had in my teams and their ability to achieve brilliant levels of performance, I knew they could fly above the traditional mind-set and performance.

We've talked about setting goals and liberating people with ownership and love. In this process, the leader has faith that his or her people can do anything—*anything*. Don't accept humdrum, mundane, boring goal setting. As your people are called upon to meet quantum performance goals, it brings out the best in them and lets them feel the thrill of soaring above the ordinary.

They truly are flying and will continue to achieve if the experience is a shared adventure with them, you, and their teammates. In that way, their daily efforts are focused on the vision and reward is earned by making it come alive. Fly high and people naturally move into their potential because success gives them such confidence and power.

## BELIEF IN SELF AND TEAM

Belief in self is the fundamental platform for accomplishment in business and life. A good hiring manager will recognize that attribute in anyone she interviews and will develop a team in which this value is consistent.

Belief in self starts with believing that there is a reason for you to be here in this universe, there is a reason God has chosen you to walk this very journey. You have to work toward a place where you believe in yourself as much as God believes in you. I don't know if you ever get there, but I think that it's the journey that counts.

If you truly search for the divine spark in others, you treat them differently. There is a reason that you are here, and that reason is far more than you can even imagine or comprehend. Even though you can't define it, deep down in your heart and soul, you know. Is it any accident that you are living your life here on earth at this time? I don't think so, do you? And if you really think and meditate on it, you will grasp the significance of your life. This is an incredibly important spiritual power in your life.

Seeking God, seeking your true potential, and seeking your place in this universe are constant challenges for all of us. One of the benefits of maintaining a spiritual approach is that your perspective is governed from a higher level—that of seeing the Divinity in yourself, in others, and in life.

With that view, love becomes the dominant factor. It allows you to evolve into the state of actualization. Your job is to grow yourself *and* your people. By focusing on the potential of each member of your team, you propel yourself and your team to a higher level.

Now that we've had this philosophical discussion regarding empowerment, let's take another look at managerial applications such as compensation, performance reviews, management process, and managing expenses, which should reflect the principles we've talked about.

## COMPENSATION

I first ensured our financial package and fringe benefits were competitive based on what our industry termed "excellent performance." Of course, my focus was on achieving the quantum level. That's where the real upside exists for the company and the individual. We included built-in accelerators once the quantum level was achieved and, operationally, that was our total focus, as in "that's how you keep your job."

Everyone knew raises in base salary did not interest me. The way to max out compensation was all about variable incentives for quantum performance. The ultimate leverage was stock options. They were earned, not given. When someone reached the quantum level, a nice grant of stock options was waiting. I was able to project the potential value of the grant based on our vision and financial model. That was the ultimate avenue for the individual to change his quality of life dramatically and provide all the material comforts for his family.

## PERFORMANCE REVIEWS

Here's an exciting subject—maybe to the human resources office—but certainly to no one else. I bring this up because there is a way to give some character to what is normally considered drudgery by all involved.

The best thing is not to have performance reviews. If a manager is doing his job, the employee will know exactly where she stands at all times. Who needs a performance review?

Here's the way the performance review process normally goes. The HR notices it's time for the manager to do a performance review on an employee. The manager puts aside the notice and doesn't do anything with the form until the last minute because he hates doing it. After several reminders from personnel, the manager finally takes a rushed look at the form to get it over with. He calls in the employee for her performance review. With a good manager, the employee should already know where she stands, so she doesn't want to waste a lot of time on this either. She just wants to know if she's getting a raise.

I came to believe that the enthusiasm of a manager for this process was inversely correlated with his acumen and competence as an effective leader. When managers talked about enjoying doing performance reviews, a red flag went up for me.

Okay, so your company mistakenly requires performance reviews, and you can't get out of it. What do you do?

I simply gave the form to the employee and asked him to fill it out because he knew better than anyone how he was doing. When I first started doing this, it threw people off. But after a while, the employees really got a kick out of this process. I found they were typically tougher on themselves than I would be. It was ironic that I would break every rule of the process and then wind up telling people they were too hard on themselves. Now what kind of motivation do you think that gave the employee?

A process they normally hated turned into something pretty cool. Their boss trusted them to fill out the form, and he would tell them if they were too tough on themselves. On the subject of salary increases, I would ask for their input "as a shareholder." What I liked to do was give more stock options in lieu of raises. This approach takes the courage to believe in your employees totally, a radical concept to some. It also takes loving your people enough to give them creative license to do their thing—and they will with heart and soul.

## THE MANAGEMENT PROCESS

Let me describe the process I used to lead a $1.6 billion international field organization that was soaring like a rocket ship. My management team consisted of seven vice presidents who covered the Americas, the Pacific Rim, Europe, Australia, and South America.

On the first of the month, we would gather at our headquarters in California. We had a simple, one-page format for providing each vice president with his quantum financial goals for the month and quarter spread on a weekly basis. We discussed any major operational issues as a team. Then we'd go out and have fun. Every Monday morning for the rest of the month, we had a worldwide teleconference. Each VP would update us on his progress toward his key financial goals, month to date. I literally kept the numbers for the month and quarter in a small section of my daybook.

During the month, my advice to the team was, "Do what you think is right and what you think our shareholders would want you to do. Don't call me unless you really need my help. I know you and trust that you will always do the right thing, especially considering the sacred responsibility we have to our company, employees, and shareholders."

That was basically the entire management process. Knowing how to delegate is the ultimate win-win in management disciplines. Yet most senior managers have a real problem with this. They think they know how to do everything better than everyone else so they try to do just that. I actually believe some executives subconsciously hire marginal staff so they can demonstrate their prowess in all the functional areas under their control. It gives their shaky ego a "boost" and allows them to demonstrate their expertise to all. It's a horribly misguided power trip.

The management process is simple. You hire a quality team. You provide them a vision of where you want to go and a set of clearly defined objectives. Then you GET OUT OF THEIR WAY! They know you're there for them if they need you. They also know you have the ultimate confidence in them to take you to the top of the mountain. They have the great feeling of empowerment, and you have the time to concentrate on your key responsibilities, like ensuring they all know they're loved and cared for.

## MANAGING EXPENSES: COUNT PEOPLE, NOT PENCILS

Too often, the corporate bean counters (my friends in the financial department) focus on nominal costs and create frustration for everyone. You literally have to sit them down and talk about the ramifications of their actions. The real costs in any company are personnel expenses: headcount, compensation, benefits, etc. Management needs to focus on headcount and productivity. That's where the real payoff in profitability is. We need to discourage bean counters from driving people nuts with petty expenses that have little impact on the bottom line.

A friend of mine worked as a reporter for a major metropolitan newspaper at which the accountants decided too much was being spent on office supplies. To save money, the office manager would sign out two legal pads and two pens at a time to the reporters. Can you imagine the insult to these resourceful, creative journalists who drove the success of that paper?

Empathize with the people who have to deal with this kind of annoyance. Teach those well-meaning financial people who don't know any better. They have skills and talents, so enroll them in the higher purpose of supporting quantum performance. Give them some stock options so they can think about the bigger picture.

Your job as a leader is to empower your people, eliminate obstacles, and provide a breathtaking presence, vision, and inspiration. Don't accept shortsighted practices and policies that insult your people. They will love you for it.

## Chapter Summary

- Empowerment includes financial, psychological, and operational issues. Equity in the form of stock options underscores a sense of responsibility and accountability and should be given to ALL employees.

- Salaries make statements, but the real upside comes with variable compensation based on quantum performance.

- Develop a mind-set within your employees that they, in fact, are leaders and have responsibility for the company's success. You want to create a collective leadership that involves everyone.

- Start to see your customers as members of the team. You want them to own your success.

- Managerial disciplines such as performance reviews, management process, and managing expenses must be governed by the principles of empowerment and ownership.

# CHAPTER 7

# TRANSCEND TO THE HIGHER LEVEL

*"What a man can be, he must be."*
*Abraham Maslow*

I mentioned Viktor Frankl's *Man's Search for Meaning* in Chapter 3 as what I consider the most profound book ever written. It exemplifies how powerful love is no matter what the circumstance. He was a prominent psychiatrist in Vienna who lost his family in Auschwitz. He writes about the power of love even in the hell he and others suffered. He champions those who marched into the ovens with their heads held high and a prayer in their hearts. This can put into perspective our ability to transcend the most unimaginable challenges life presents. It redefines and puts into context the everyday issues we face in the business world.

## THE SPIRITUAL CAPITALIST PERSPECTIVE

Leaders don't blame others—or the universe—for their problems. They never whine about life being unfair. Most people think, if I just get past this problem, everything will be OK. The Spiritual Capitalist understands that happiness and peace come from knowing that whatever problem arises, he can solve it. You have to learn to enjoy the problems. It's supposed to be hard; that's what makes it so much fun and so lucrative.

Once you convert to this mind-set, you work with a whole different attitude. Transcending the norm, transcending the fear, you operate in a Zenlike zone. You recognize that the world is made up of different people. There are the few who make it happen and the many that don't. There are the few who take responsibility and the many who don't. There are the few who come from a place of love and the many who don't.

In business, expectations must be managed and your people need to understand why the reward for quantum performance can be so intrinsically fulfilling and financially rewarding is because in the real world there is no such thing as perfection. Problems will arise with products, marketing, customer service, support departments, and other areas of your company's operation.

When I heard someone in our sales organization moan about some problem we had, I would explain we were lucky these problems existed, as they always will. Our people needed to understand that they made the big bucks based on their ability to manage the situation, no matter the problem or issue.

The difference in perspective shows up when we compare our old friend, the Traditional Regressive, with our hero, the Spiritual Capitalist:

| TRADITIONAL REGRESSIVE | SPIRITUAL CAPITALIST |
|---|---|
| I'll lowball goals | I'm committed to quantum performance |
| It wasn't my fault | I'll take responsibility for that |
| The product was screwed up | I'll manage the situation |
| Lousy marketing support | I'll manage the situation |
| You screwed up | Let me help you |
| No way | I'll make it happen |
| I never get a break | I make my own breaks |
| What about the policy manual? | Screw the policy manual |
| What about me? | What about them? |
| I'll need to justify this | I'll do what's right |
| Politically incorrect | Forget the politics |
| Look at the effort I made | Look at my results |
| I need to plan this out | I'm acting now on my gut |
| I can't handle this | I'll find a way |
| I can't | I can |
| Life's unfair | Life is a grand adventure |

## SELF-ACTUALIZATION

When I reflect on the title of this chapter, I immediately go back to Maslow's Hierarchy of Needs, which so powerfully defines the logic and power behind Spiritual Capitalism. As we've discussed, the Traditional Regressive setting satisfies only the bottom two levels of the pyramid, physiological and safety needs. A culture of Spiritual Capitalism allows the individual to transcend into the ultimate place of self-actualization.

## QUANTUM PERFORMANCE

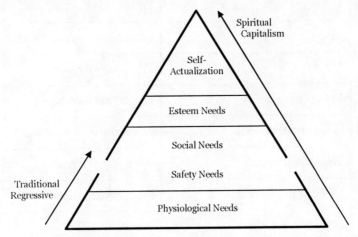

## TRANSCEND THE B.S.

The business world is full of b.s. that cripples it and chokes performance. Office politics, rules, policies, procedures, regulations, directives, memorandums, reports, e-mail (I hate e-mail), and the like literally drown employees. One must step back and play at a higher level. Look at all of that damned paperwork and determine for yourself and your team what will be addressed and what will be ignored. If you and your team are performing at an optimal level, you have the leverage to make those determinations yourself.

In terms of office politics, business is rampant with people who brownnose and jockey for position. You have to understand what drives that kind of behavior. Typically, it's our old friends fear and insecurity. The leader

---

### Engaged Employees

*Leave it to the consultants to quantify emotion. The Gallup Organization has turned the psychological benefits of Spiritual Capitalism into a consulting bonanza by going into companies to determine how "engaged" employees are with their jobs. Gallup surveys employees on twelve issues to see how their job satisfaction affects their likelihood of exceeding expectations. The theory is if you are engaged, you'll do more.*

*So employees are surveyed on whether they know what is expected of them, if they have close friends at work, if they have recently been praised for their performance. The more positive the responses, the more engaged the employee. The more engaged the employee, the more likely the person will achieve at a quantum level of performance. Do you really need a survey to tell you whether people are happy and fulfilled at work? No! Quantum performance is a natural by-product of the loving and empowering approach of the Spiritual Capitalist. It's so simple, but corporations are paying millions to learn the free lessons of the heart.*

must determine if such an individual is capable of performing at the team's level. If so, the team envelops that individual and he or she moves away from the fray toward the level of self-actualization.

You need to sharpen your view of things and know the few real critical priorities. That is where your focus must be, and anything that impedes those activities must be eradicated.

Paperwork cripples. Sometimes you just have to say, "No, I'm not doing this. It adds no value to my operation. It encumbers my people." If you are operating in a traditional company that cherishes its policies and procedures, you have to challenge other leaders to decide whether the paperwork and formality is really required if it is ultimately costing dollars and success. You do that by enrolling them in your vision and, in so doing, you liberate them. If you get resistance, you can say, "I want you to prove to me that this is a valuable activity. I'll listen and, after the discussion, I'll make the decide whether or not we'll do what is requested."

That can be tough, and especially takes courage when you are a middle manager. But if you put it in context by saying, "I'm at 200% of our goal, and we are the top achievers in this company. I have a few critical activities that I focus on to ensure this level of performance. Now this request for a report does not meet my criteria for critical activities, and I haven't had anyone explain the value of it to me." It's an incredibly empowering experience.

## NO NEED FOR EXCUSES

One of my favorite sayings is, "Don't confuse efforts with results." Some people want to spend a lot of time telling you how hard they worked, how many hours they spent on the project, and the problems they encountered. They need to understand that the bottom line is the results. I have found that, paradoxically, those who seemingly work fewer hours produce more when they are involved in a quantum performance environment.

People give excuses to explain away nonperformance. They have an agreed-upon goal and, if they don't meet it, they provide you with excuses. They imply that the lack of performance was out of their control. This is where the manager or leader constructively confronts the individual and underscores that the focus is on results, not excuses. Once the employee takes that in, a whole new mind-set is established.

When you are operating in the higher realm, excuses from your people become irrelevant. Your team members know that everyone is doing everything in his or her power to reach the higher level of self- and team-actualization. There is a belief in one another, a collective self-confidence. There is knowledge of the competency of each individual.

Excuse making is a habit learned over the years and driven by fear and insecurity. Once the team member feels loved and embraced, the need for excuse making dissolves. Everyone knows that everyone else is giving his or her very best. If things go wrong, the problems are simply identified and examined, so a solution can be devised. The elimination of excuses saves a lot of unproductive time that can be redirected to problem resolution. It also gives every team member the license to say, "I'm sorry," "I screwed up," "This is an issue that I need help on."

What a liberating environment! It promotes the individual's evolution and has eliminated the need to fabricate "reasons why" something didn't work. The employees' focus can then be on results.

## MANAGERIAL APPLICATIONS

Now that we've discussed the philosophical background, let's touch briefly on some of the managerial disciplines that should be guided by the principles we've talked about.

- You don't accept the unacceptable. Rather than constantly rationalizing nonperformance, you employ the art of constructive confrontation to demand your employee transcend to a level above excuses and BS.

- You articulate a bold and daring vision that inspires people to a level of achievement they never dreamt possible.

- You establish a top-down quantum goal-setting process that stretches your people into greatness versus the limiting tradition of bottom-up forecasting.

Our realistic view of the business world, with all its problems and challenges, presents us the opportunity to believe in ourselves and to grow into who we really are. Excuses, blame, lack of accountability, and, yes, all the BS are left for others to wallow in until they awaken and discover their true identity. Hopefully, an enlightened leader will come into their life and, through the power of love, take them to a higher place.

## Chapter Summary

- Leaders don't blame others—or the universe—for their problems. They never whine about life being unfair, and don't waste time or diminish themselves with excuse making.

- Office politics, rules, policies, procedures, regulations, directives, memorandums, reports, and the like literally drown leaders and employees. Step back and play at a higher level.

- The great leader focused on taking his team and company to a quantum level of performance does not accept the unacceptable and uses constructive confrontation to demand his people go there with him.

- A perspective that transcends all the traditional "norms" guides great vision and quantum goal setting.

- The bottom line is the results. Great teams operate on a higher level above all the excuses and BS that limits others.

# CHAPTER 8

# DON'T TAKE IT ALL SO SERIOUSLY

*"Work is good, provided you do not forget to live."*
*Old Hindu Proverb*


Lorin Maazel, in his 70s, is the music director of the New York Philharmonic and a legend in the world of music. He believes the great leader gives up the need for control in exchange for freedom, creativity, and love. He provides his people a lightness of spirit that encourages them to strive for excellence and passion knowing that this commitment to themselves will ultimately take them to where they belong.

Mr. Maazel is an artistic genius who also reflects an intuitive managerial genius. His concept of "lightness in spirit" is empowering and really hits home with me. It underscores the concept of not taking it all so seriously, a paradox in that it actually liberates potential.


## WORKAHOLISM

We all know the guy who treats his job as life and death. Every activity is very serious, he works 65 hours a week, and, due to exhaustion, has little time for anything else—like play or loved ones. "You don't understand; I have to do it" is the mantra he lives by, if you can call it living.

Some shallow senior executives actually believe this approach to the job is admirable and encourage, mandate, or dictate it. These managers and their employees have it all wrong. They don't understand that there is in fact an inverse relationship between hours slaving at work and productivity.

The person who works all those hours is putting lots of pressure on himself. He has to do everything himself because he's a control freak and, in truth, is very insecure and full of fear. He is mentally exhausted. His whole identity is wrapped up in the job. He's not happy in his life and has external family pressures.

The typical workaholic is not realizing his or her potential. The leader's objective in work is to have the vision, know the way, lead his team, achieve results, have fun, and position himself for a balanced and happy life. Once you cross the line into workaholism, compulsion, and obsession, your results suffer commensurately.

The manager who finds himself in this trap typically does not have the right people on the team; he has not done a good job of hiring and firing and has failed to define a precise vision of where the team is headed. He does not have a lean and responsive management process. Most important, this "leader" has not empowered the team members by showing confidence in them and giving them latitude and flexibility in getting their jobs done.

When a manager talked to me about how hard he was working each week, a red flag always appeared in my mind.

## THE SPIRITUAL CAPITALIST PERSPECTIVE

As a Spiritual Capitalist, you set it up with the right empowered people who get your vision, and you work less, achieve more, and suffer less stress. Because you're not a slave to your job and you lead an empowered team, you maintain a balanced life of love, play, work, and spirituality. And you don't take it all so seriously.

You believe things happen for a reason, that there are always alternatives if needed. You know many times in your life trauma left hidden blessings. You have a sense of the bigger picture of life. You've also adopted the powerful psychological habit of asking yourself, "What's the worst-case scenario in this situation?" This technique can immediately put you at ease and things in perspective. Nine times out of ten, whatever that worst-case scenario might be, you've handled worse situations.

It is that simple.

Which approach do you think is more productive? Which person do you think is happier and has more fun? Which one do you think has more love in his or her life?

If you are working 60 or 70 hours a week, you need to step back and ask yourself what is wrong. Work backward to pinpoint the fundamental operational problems that are keeping you from achieving quantum performance with minimal stress. What's the problem? The players on your team? Your game plan? Its execution?

Something has to change. Working those kinds of hours is a signal that something is fundamentally wrong. The alarm should be going off in your head right now. You're not living right. Look at the cross of balance that we'll discuss later in this chapter, which addresses mind, body, soul, and heart. What needs to change, and how are you going to change it?

## INSPIRE TEAM MEMBERS TO BE THERE FOR ONE ANOTHER

In too many situations, business is looked at as a life-or-death prospect. It ain't the ER! When you lighten up, have fun, and come from a place of love in your dealings with your people and your customers, exceptional performance results. Another side of fear and insecurity in terms of senior management is the lack of a sense of humor. If you take business too seriously, you'll impede the potential for enormous success. In terms of the bond with your team, a light touch goes a long way.

When you see someone walking around the office with a deadly serious look on his or her face, tension in the body, and an inability to smile, you'll find someone who will never achieve his or her potential. Reach your people by sitting down with them and talking with them: "You're going around all tensed up, looking like it's life or death. It's not. We're going to do the best we can. We're going to go for it. If it doesn't work, we'll think of something else. But I think you are the best and you have a team around you that will support you. So talk to me about any fear you have about your ability to contribute to this company. Don't hold back. If you keep it tied up in a bundle of tension and stress, you won't do anyone any good." Most people will open up with relief.

I used to say to that person, "Hey, everyone is coming into the office today. We're going to go out and have dinner, a few drinks, and we're going to let you know how much we love you and that we've talked and there are some things that are bugging you that you need to get out on the table for the team. We need to talk about it with you, so you can achieve your potential."

We'd have the dinner and say: "We are glad you are on this team, we want to support you, and we know there are some things that are bothering you. Let's get it out there; let's come up with a plan to address it. We're behind you all the way."

Every once in a while I'd walk into someone's office and he'd have that look of being overwhelmed. I'd ask what the problem was. The typical response was, "Look at all this paperwork on my desk. I'll never get it all done." I'd simply give him a knowing smile, take all the paperwork off the desk, throw it in the wastebasket, and tell him, "Don't sweat it. If it's really important, you'll hear about it." His response was something like, "My God." You know, at that point, I'd feel like a god (small g). I had set them free.

It was that simple—and that powerful.


## LIGHTEN UP

In my first job as a sales manager, we had a really loud and obnoxious boat horn at our receptionist's desk. It served an important purpose in recognizing excellence and our team's esprit de corps. When a salesman came into the office with an order worth at least $500,000, the boat horn would sound. This signaled everyone to wrap up anything they were doing because it was party time. Refreshments were brought in, a camera was brought out, and we all serenaded our conquering hero.

Once an HR person was visiting my office in Atlanta. Among other things, he mentioned that word was getting around about our parties in the office. Sure enough, the boat horn sounded and he stood in amazement at the energy in the office. He looked at me, then went out and looked at us. He gave me a smile, had a glass of refreshment, and joined in the fun—an immediate convert. I heard when he visited other offices, he would actually tell our story and recommend they do the same. Funny how a little fun and love can affect the "straightest arrow."

Sometimes I'd detect a little lethargy creeping into the office, so I'd put on my Rollerblades, get my baseball bat, and go raise some hell. I'm not kidding. I'd glide through the building from department to department, and laughter would fill the place.

First stop would be manufacturing. I'd pound the end of the bat on the desk of the V.P. of manufacturing and shout, "When are you guys going to get off your butts and get those products out? Why are we so slow with delivery dates? We've got this sales machine that's on fire, and you guys need to get off your asses!"

The whole place would lose it with laughter because they knew I was just having fun with them, caring about them, and laughing with them. The next stop was Bernie, the VP of marketing. "HELLOOO, BERNIE! How about a little marketing support? When are you going to get your act together?"

If I wanted to be sure I got everyone's attention, I would regale everybody at the top of my voice with what had to be the absolute worst example of "singing" country music. I would literally be booed out of the building. You've got to laugh as you lead. In fact, these are some of my favorite memories.

It may not be your style to Rollerblade through your office, but the point is to put everything in its proper context. If you keep that in mind, you'll find that when a report is two days late, it really isn't the end of the world. When the product doesn't work right, the planet is not going to stop revolving. When you have lost a sale, life does not end. If a customer screams and yells at you, the sun will rise again tomorrow.

Those problems are temporary although sometimes difficult, but once you adopt the philosophical perspective that life does not begin or end based on what happens in a day at the office, you gain the power to enjoy what you are doing and perform better. Believe me, if you think getting a sale is the end of the world you'll have less of a chance of closing it than the salesman who gives it his best shot, does everything possible to get the order, yet maintains the philosophical perspective that it is not life or death.

## STRESS AND WORK

The fundamental cause of stress in the work environment is the inability for a company to achieve its goals. Failure is a paralyzing agent in life and in work. So, the first order of business is to ensure your company and your team are poised for success.

From a company point of view, are you in a good, strong market and do you have competitive products and services? If so, the variable comes down to managerial excellence and leadership. Where people are achieving in a Spiritual Capitalist environment, stress is mitigated. It's every manager's job to ensure his or her team is succeeding in making its contribution to the company's success. If you find yourself in a stressful place, ask yourself:

1. Is my company positioned for success?

2. Do I feel a strong, caring bond with my boss and my team?

3. In honest self-analysis, do I know that I have the ability to do the job that is required of me?

If the answer is no to any of these questions, then you need to find an environment that matches your skill set and provides you with a feeling of joy and achievement in your work.

Sometimes, you just have to lighten up. If you are with a good company with good products and good management, you have to sit back and look at the big picture. It is *not* life and death. That's your mantra. You can't perform to your greatest potential if you let your insecurities paralyze you. And one of the greatest ways of letting that happen is losing perspective on the full picture of your life. We all do it, but we must consciously incorporate the work-life-balance issues into our everyday life.

No job is worth a heart attack.

## THERE ARE ALWAYS ALTERNATIVES

One of the ways that we trap ourselves into a desperate perspective is by forgetting there are always alternatives. Specifically, in the context of Spiritual Capitalism, there is always another company, there is always another position, and there is always another boss. There is always another way for you to realize your true potential. Locking yourself into a situation is self-sabotaging. All we can do is the best we can do, and if you aren't realizing your full potential, then it is incumbent on you to find another situation that promotes that.

This knowledge that there are, in fact, alternatives, can typically give you a feeling of freedom and flexibility. Go find another job! Find something you are great at. Don't suffer through this misery. You always have the option to fire your boss, and that is empowering and liberating. Hopefully, you don't have to, but just knowing that you can walk will remind you that you are not chained to your current situation. You just aren't. You are fully capable of using your skills and talents wherever you land.

When you are unhappy, unfulfilled, and feeling you aren't realizing your potential, it's time to seek new alternatives. When it is no fun, when you hate going to work, or the energy is negative, it's time. If it's "just a job" rather than a path to your potential, it's time.

People tell themselves, "At least I've got a job," and are sometimes afraid to pursue other opportunities because they may be rejected in the process. Some may lack the confidence to prove themselves again in another environment. Seek out a mentor, friend, minister, counselor, or therapist, and get an outside perspective that will guide you to make changes. Choose to be the person you want to be. Define it, articulate it, write it down, and use it as a guide. Don't let that neurotic voice inside your head tell you, "Oh, I can't leave this job. I hate it, but I probably can't get anything better. At least I know this. It may be miserable, but I know what's here. I don't know what's out there."

Confront that insecurity by redefining yourself and committing yourself, second by second if necessary, to becoming the person who represents your ideal. When you need courage, you can find it from your friends, your family, your counselor, and your God. Build the support you need and decide to be the person you want to be. Take steps that will allow you to flourish as that person.

As the wise ones tell us, courage is not a lack of fear. Courage is acting in the presence of fear.

## SEE THE HUMOR IN THINGS

Life is full of humor, if we have the awareness to experience it. A touch of humor helps with priorities. A light touch has tremendous power. Those who take everything deadly seriously are typically underperformers. They are the workaholics and the 65-hour-a-week martyrs. Relax! Stand back. See everything for what it truly is. Know that a sense of humor is one of the most important attributes in business and life.

Look for humor. Bring a perspective of lightness with a positive attitude. Searching for the lighter dimension of the situation can, in fact, energize you and your people.

Consciously find that which is light, funny, invigorating, and contagious. When the mood turns dour, brighten it up by reminding your people that it isn't as serious as it seems. It just isn't.

We always tried to keep things lively and fun in our boardroom. Our board was composed of very successful investors and senior executives. All were multimillionaires, except for two billionaires. They were very pleased with our performance. You can imagine the rush this old cotton picker got when I entered the room and they did the bow-down act recognizing our success and the tremendous return received on their investments in our company.

So I decided to have a little fun with them. In a stern and solemn voice, I told them how much I enjoyed and appreciated the experience we'd had together. I thanked them for their support and the fortune I had made. But I told them I had received a compelling offer from an individual I could not name who had offered me an opportunity to pursue a dream I'd had all my life. The shock and dismay on their faces was palpable.

After waiting in a silent and stunned room for what seemed like a couple of minutes, I told them I could show them a picture depicting my new venture. With that, I whipped out a picture of my new partner and me with arms around each other.

It was Michael Jordan and me. I had just returned from the camp he has in Las Vegas for middle-aged men who still think they can play basketball. Not. That got the most laughter I think I've ever heard in a board meeting.

For billionaires, or whomever, humor is the language that unites and brings a gracious and light feeling of love with it.

## THE REALLY BIG PICTURE

I think about dying and meeting God. What is God going to be concerned about? Is it going to be that report you are stressing over, that raise or promotion you didn't get? Is God going to care about that meeting you missed? I don't think so. What God will be concerned with, particularly in the work context, is whether or not you came from a place of love. Whether you were kind and caring to your employees. That you genuinely wanted the best for them, and you were there for them in times of trouble. That you smiled and laughed and enjoyed the whole crazy experience of life.

You have to come to that awareness. Something has to spark your mind so you can look at it, digest it, and live it. That way you can modify your behavior accordingly. When I see somebody really uptight I go, "Chill, man!" And it hits them, "What am I so upset about?"

In each chapter, we've discussed managerial applications that illustrate the particular commandment, i.e., the managerial principle. The following is one of my favorites in terms of not taking it all too seriously.

## DON'T DO E-MAIL

Want to free up at least ten hours each week? Want to get a 10% boost in productivity? Want to experience a less hassled week? Want to eliminate superfluous communications? Want to empower your employees? Want to spend more quality time with your family? Want to save valuable brain cells?

Quit e-mailing! I know that may sound sacrilegious or impractical in today's world. But who cares, if you can get the type of payoff I've experienced.

I came to this dramatic conclusion because of exhaustion. I'd fly into a city late at night, check into the hotel, and first review my voice mail because of its real-time orientation. Then came the joy of checking e-mail.

After about an hour of attempting to get connected to the home office server, I would gaze in puzzled amazement as I categorized them into:

- Who is this person?
- What a bunch of BS!
- I wonder how long this took to write?
- What a brownnoser.
- Total CYA.
- Who cares?
- Duh.

One morning, I told the employees in our company that I was quitting e-mail. "No way," they said. "You can't do that!" and, "How will we operate?" You would have thought our business was e-mailing each other all day. Boy, did I get a rise, but I was adamant in my position.

E-mail breeds a CYA electronic maze that prevents people from being proactive. The majority of e-mail messages are not of a critical, time-sensitive nature. Experience shows that employees spend an average of one to two hours checking, responding to, and writing approximately 130 e-mails EACH DAY. Studies suggest over 50% of e-mails are incorrectly interpreted by the receiver, and most people vastly overestimate their ability to relay and comprehend messages accurately.

As International Association of Business Communicators President Julie Freeman notes in a recent *BusinessWeek* article, "Most corporate policies are aimed at protecting the e-mail system rather than helping you be an effective communicator."

The peoples of the earth sent and received 400,000 terabytes of information by e-mail in 2002, according to research by the University of California at Berkeley's School of Information. That's equivalent to the print collections of 40,000 Libraries of Congress. And that was measured way back in 2002: The quantity has grown dramatically since.

In a company with 1,000 people, this translates into losing 1,000 to 2,000 hours per day on this energy-draining activity. Imagine approaching a CEO with an idea to expend 1,000 to 2,000 man-hours each day at a cost of more than $1.5 million per month with little return on investment.

My team could always come see me, call me in the office or on my cell phone, or leave a voice mail. If we didn't connect, I promised I would respond to voice mail within twelve hours. I much prefer verbal and voice-mail communication because of its more personal and real-time orientation and the great savings in time compared to e-mail.

And every Tom, Dick, and Harry can't access your voice-mail number like they can your e-mail address. Pretty sick of spam and junk e-mail?

We had a simple set of guidelines on decisions that needed to be reviewed by me. If somehow we failed to connect, and if the decision had to be made in real-time (few do), I told them just to do the right thing.

Within two weeks of my new policy, I began experiencing the benefits of saving ten hours per week, a real boost in productivity, no more time-consuming e-mail that really didn't say anything, clearer communication with my employees, and more quality time with my family. On the other end, our employees felt more empowered, appreciated the personal nature of our communication, and were liberated from the destructive mentality e-mail can promote.

Free yourself from this addictive electronic "tool" and save money, increase productivity, and empower your people. I heard the other day that some are literally considering a 12-Step recovery program to liberate people from this obsession. My perspective is just another example of Spiritual (empowering and liberating people) Capitalism (saving money and increasing productivity).

If you're hesitant, just ignore your e-mail for a couple of weeks and see what happens. Trust me, you'll hear about the really important things. The only general exception to this policy I can think of is customers who want to communicate via e-mail.

## STRATEGIC BUSINESS PLANS

I always chuckle when people get all worked up about the absolute necessity that a long, boring, weighty "strategic business plan" is a life-or-death issue.

When someone mentions strategic business plans, I immediately think of a weight scale. They theoretically cover five years and weigh about five pounds. And they're usually a bunch of BS. Who in the hell can see out that far? Nonline "staffers" are the major sources of "input." This useless exercise is futile and costs a lot of time and money to produce little real value. The rule of inverse correlation applies: The thicker the business plan, the higher the probability of failure.

We focused on a twelve-month game plan, broken down into projected monthly and quarter financials, which were something you could really get your teeth in. The general format included:

- Our five strategic goals with a focus on financial projections
- Quantum revenue growth with 25% operating margins
- The five tactical initiatives associated with each of our strategic goals
- Defined individual responsibilities and time frames.

Have you asked yourself the truly salient questions for planning future success?

- How are you positioned in terms of market and product?
- Do you have a compelling vision that takes people's breath away?
- Have you written a brief mission statement that reflects your vision and put it on everyone's desk?

- Have you given everyone an equity stake and told each of them what it will add up to if he or she achieves your major goals?

- Have you built the right team?

- What about market segment focus and distribution strategy?

- How powerful is your sales team at relationship selling?

- Do your products give you a high gross margin?

- Do you have inspiring leadership and meticulous managerial execution?

- Have you developed a high-performance culture?

Spend your time honestly and critically addressing these questions and developing a lean and precise twelve-month game plan.

If you're focused on truthfully answering these questions and making this game plan happen, trust me—the future will take care of itself.

## WHAT'S IT ALL ABOUT?

In too many situations, business is seen as a life-or-death proposition. Again, it ain't the ER! Once your company is properly positioned in terms of market and product, you've developed the right team and high-performance culture, and you lighten up, have fun, and come from a place of love, you've created the basics for exceptional performance.

If you don't have these basics in place, you're in need of radical transformation. If that seems impossible, I'd look for another company, at which this environment exists or is feasible. Don't forget that there are always alternatives if your needs can't be met by your current employer. I've always felt the lack of a sense of lightness and humor in a company is just another sign of fear and insecurity. It creates a stifling situation in which genuine growth is hopeless.

Also, keep the cosmic perspective somewhere in your consciousness to address your problems' relative importance in the fabric of your life. If something is not going to matter in three months, is it worth so much worry today? Just buckle up, and get beyond it. Few issues deserve the life-and-death importance we seem to assign them.

In the end, what really matters?

I once sat on a boulder hanging out over the Snake River in Idaho on a retreat with one of the most prominent psychiatrists in the world. He and I had established an immediate rapport, when he found out who I was and told me about the incredible return he had enjoyed as a shareholder in my company.

We were on a river-rafting expedition and had stopped for the evening. I asked him what he thought life was all about. After some time reflecting on my question, he told me it was about how you feel about yourself when you lay your head on the pillow at night and how you'll feel in old age when you know death is near. Your thoughts at night on that pillow center on reviewing the life you've led.

## INNER PEACE

Let's face it—the ultimate objective of life is inner peace and happiness. So what are the "symptoms" of inner peace?

- A tendency to think and act spontaneously rather than on fears based on past experiences.

- An unmistakable ability to enjoy each moment.

- A loss of the ability to worry.

- Frequent, overwhelming episodes of appreciation.

- Contented feelings of connectedness with others and nature.

- Frequent attacks of smiling.

- An increasing tendency to let things happen rather than make them happen.

## A BALANCED LIFE

All of the great masters tell us that the key to happiness is living a balanced life. Appreciate that God gave us a heart to love with, a mind to think with, a soul to guide us on our spiritual path, and a body for the physical dimension of this material world of ours. So to find happiness, you've got to balance the mind (i.e., work), the heart (i.e., love), the body (i.e., play), and the soul (i.e., worship). People are always in danger working 60 or 70 hours a week because they aren't giving enough attention to the other dimensions of their lives.

If you balance these aspects of your life, you will bring yourself happiness. The unbalanced life of a workaholic leads to disaster. If you have no personal life, family life, love life, or play life, you are living a one-dimensional existence that doesn't count for much.

It's not the number of hours you work; it's the results you produce. Don't get confused between the two. Many times I have seen someone work 70 hours a week struggling to come close to his or her objectives, while someone else is working 40 hours a week and handling the challenge with ease. A balanced life gives you the energy and perspective you need to accomplish great things.

I saw the following Cross of Balance someplace and it has always resonated with me. It can be a kind of guide for you. If you can balance your life and pay attention to each of the four dimensions of the cross, chances are you'll be rewarded with a happier life.

## CROSS OF BALANCE

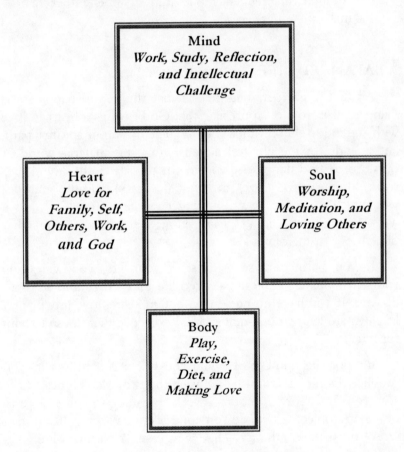

I know it's easy to say but challenging to live this way. The people I know who come closest are the happiest. If you feel like you're drowning, all the fun has gone out of life, you work and work and just don't get there, and there seems to be no way out—there is.

Meditate on this cross, then be brave, believe in yourself, and change the way you're living. If you can transform yourself in your current situation, go for it. If you can't, get out and find a better fit in which you can live life the way God wants you to.

Amen.

## Chapter Summary

- Once you cross the line into workaholism, compulsion, and obsession, your results suffer commensurately.

- There is incredible power in a lightness of spirit and the ability to inject humor into practically any situation.

- To find happiness, you've got to balance the mind (i.e., work), the heart (i.e., love), the body (i.e., play), and the soul (i.e., worship).

- The fundamental cause of stress at work is a company's inability to achieve its goals. Failure is a paralyzing agent in life and work. So the first order of business is to ensure your company is positioned for success.

- Lighten up on the e-mail and "strategic business plans." Real communication and simple, powerful game plans will take you there.

- There is always another company, another position, and another boss. There is always another way for you to realize your true potential.

# CHAPTER 9

## COUNT YOUR BLESSINGS

*"Gratitude is not only the greatest of virtues but the parent of all the others."* - *Cicero*

We all are heavily influenced by our parents, our upbringing, our genetics, and our environment. I always felt like I got a double dose. I survived horrible beatings in a poor and brutal small town in Tennessee where we lived in a "house" with no plumbing, water, or electricity. We had an outhouse for a toilet. My job at the age of 6 was picking cotton all day long. My father finally committed suicide, and I pray that poor soul has found peace in the next life.

My mother was a different story. She did everything around the house while working crazy shifts at a factory in Memphis to put bread on our table. She was a devout, fun-loving Christian and talked about Jesus like he lived around the corner.

They say how you die says a lot about how you lived. Since I was making good money, I was able to give my mother anything she wanted over the last ten years of her life. When we knew my Mom was close to death, my youngest daughter and I stayed with her the last few weeks of her life.

You would have never believed someone was about to die in that house. You see, most feel desperate fear when they're about to go. My mom stared death in the face and didn't blink. Friends were over, laughing and drinking, playing cards, and telling dirty jokes! I think you can see why she is a hero of mine.

I remember on her deathbed, with only a little time left, she asked that I write her eulogy. I assured her I would. After a moment of pause, she told me to write it right now. I tried to explain to her that this was typically done after the individual had deceased. "No, I want it done right now," she said, so that's what I did. I can still see her reading it with tears in her eyes and heart. She let go and died that night.

What does all this build up to, other than my sharing a priceless memory of my mother? This precious warrior, who endured a lot of pain throughout her life, kept it together with one key principle. She always said, "Honey, count your blessings, and they'll count you."

So what does that mean? And what's it doing in a book about optimizing corporate performance? It means that if you maintain an attitude of gratitude, you will be more productive and happier in general. Most people in the world look at Americans' material blessings with envy and think it must be easy for us to maintain such a positive perspective. Wrong. Many have a tendency to moan and groan, look at the glass as half empty, and blame it on somebody or something else. They take that attitude with them to the office.

## THE POWER OF GRATITUDE

A foundation of gratitude is essential to your mission as a Spiritual Capitalist.

Think about it. We can all get in a funk. We can all get depressed. We can all reach a time when life seems really tough. We can all get to a point in business where the challenges and problems seem daunting. That's OK; it's part of the game of life.

The tendency of many is to wrap themselves in negativity. It shows up like this:

"I never get a break."

"Why does everything happen to me?"

"I wish I had what he or she or everybody else has."

"I wish I were as happy as him or her or everybody else."

"This really sucks."

"Our products, marketing, or service are not as good as our competitors'."

"This is not fair."

"Life is not fair."

"We'll never make this plan."

"Blah, blah, blah."

I'm sure you get the drift and have heard or said these lines many times. The shrinks call it being a victim. And being that way takes all our power away. You would think the people uttering these things must know how destructive and self-defeating they are. But most of them are oblivious.

Occasionally, when one of my team got really stuck, I would take out my metaphorical two-by-four and knock the hell out of him—with words of love. I spelled out all the blessings he enjoyed. Then I would remind him that negativity was unacceptable with us and, if he couldn't change this destructive mind-set, he would have to leave. It's a simple conversation: "Joe, give me a break, my precious friend. You're with one of the top companies in the industry. Your job is challenging and fulfilling. You earn more than the vast majority of people in this world. You're healthy with a beautiful home and wonderful family. Rather than bitch and moan, you should be on your knees thanking God for all the blessings bestowed on you. And if you don't start doing that and cut the crap, I will fire you. Our team can't afford having someone who doesn't appreciate what we're all about."

You'll see something like a spiritual conversion before your very eyes. Old Joe is now one of your brightest stars, with a positive, make-it-happen perspective on his work, family, and health—all fueled by an attitude of gratitude.

Ah, the power of tough love.

## FOCUSING ON OUR BLESSINGS

The wise ones teach us that reflecting on all the blessings we have in life can be a wonderful catalyst to get us out of a funk and mobilize us to achieve our goals in life and business. If you don't believe me, just try this little exercise:

Stop right now, and get out a piece of paper. Write down the blessings you most cherish in your life, a gratitude list, if you will. It's not corny, it's the truth. Think about:

- Your life—It's really no accident you're here and that you have a purpose.

- Your job—Don't take it for granted.

- Your family—Need I say more?

- Your talents—Wonder sometimes where they came from?

- Your friends—What would life be without them?

- Your health—Most of us take it for granted.

- Your material comforts—Two billion people of the world live on $2 a day.

- Your God or Higher Power—Whatever the name, deep down most of us believe in a Supreme Being.

My list of gratitude includes:

1. The love of my children

2. My health

3. My children's health

4. Material comforts

5. Getting out of my childhood alive and finally recognizing its hidden blessings

6. My professional success

7. My financial success

8. Those who love me

9. The lives I've touched

10. The opportunity to study theology at a university and teach Spiritual Capitalism

Carry your gratitude list along with a letter you write to yourself describing who you want to be. As simplistic as this sounds, if you look at your list and your letter a couple of times a week and really take it into your heart, you will experience profound transformation.

Combining a foundation of gratitude with the challenging spiritual love we've talked so much about is critical in realizing the transformational benefits that come with the Spiritual Capitalist perspective.

You want to love going to work, maximize your company's performance and your earnings, live a balanced life, and laugh a lot.

You want to lose things like conflict, a lack of individual and collective self-confidence, long and stress-filled hours at work, and a self-defeating obsession with work.

## BLESSINGS FROM THE PAST

As I think back on my career, I have to smile at the blessings I received from my first boss, my first mentor, and my first customer.

When I was a 24-year-old young man with a wife and two children, I worked at a low-paying administrative job (about $800 a month) and barely got by. I had the opportunity to see the salesmen's commission checks and quickly decided I was in the wrong line of work. I began begging ours sales managers to give me a sales job. Finally, Dave Fuller, my first real mentor, agreed to give me a chance. Of course, I had no idea what I was getting myself into.

Dave sent me to a sales training class that used role-playing to simulate the real world (i.e., they busted our chops). Throughout the class, I was nervous as hell thinking there was no way I could do it. But I kept remembering those commission checks.

I went back into Dave's office after surviving the class and asked him what I should do next. I expected some great strategic advice, but he told me, "Get your ass busy with telephone calls, and go knock on some doors."

I got a couple of appointments and asked Dave what I should do when I got there. I knew as much about sophisticated computer systems—what I was supposedly "selling"—as my 3-year-old. He told me just to concern myself with asking a few intelligent questions and building rapport. Dave said the key was having the prospect do most of the talking.

"Mike, after you ask the question, I want you to do one thing," he said. He slyly smiled as he barked, "SHUT UP!"

As that great philosopher, my mom, said, "The reason God gave us two ears but only one mouth was that we should all listen more than talk." Or in the words of the profound John Wayne, "Talk low, talk slow, and don't say too much."

I also told our best sales rep, Jerry Miller, that I was concerned I'd be intimidated on my sales calls by the senior executives considering such a major capital investment. Jerry looked at me with that lovely confident smile of his and said, "Mike, just picture the guy on the toilet doing his business, just like you and me." Wow, I sure had never thought of that.

So I got my first appointment with Mr. William Harrer, chief financial officer with E&H Electric, a major electronics distributor. A couple of guys in the office who had previously called on Mr. Harrer told me he was totally committed to IBM and loved to give competitive salesmen a hard time,—just what I needed to send my already shaky "confidence" down the tubes.

Knees quivering, I arrived in the E&H lobby, praying that I wouldn't turn to jelly. Mr. Harrer was a 65-year-old senior executive and I was a 24-year-old me. When I met him, you guessed it, I thought of Jerry Miller's advice. I introduced myself and asked him a few reasonably intelligent questions, then just let him talk and talk. Toward the end of our conversation, I asked Mr. Harrer about some of the things he enjoyed doing. He told me, "I like to have lunch at the Old Stone Café and throw back a few Old Foresters." I took a big gulp and asked him if I could have the honor of hosting him once a week for lunch while my support staff conducted a survey to help determine his needs, problems, and our ability to deliver benefits.

Mr. Harrer and I became real friends during our weekly luncheon, and my company replaced IBM as his computer vendor. I loved that old man like a father and vice-versa. And I can still see my wife and I staring in disbelief at my first commission check!

I became one of the top salesmen in our company's history. As I progressed in my career, I let no one intimidate me. I know some of the lessons that I learned early on helped build the foundation for my career. I learned one should never be afraid to be unafraid. I also learned that the people who come into our life early are like gifts from God.

## THE SPIRITUAL CAPITALIST PERSPECTIVE

I've emphasized throughout this book that a spiritual perspective empowers us in our work like nothing else. We are spiritual beings experiencing a material world. Loving ourselves and others, worshipping, caring for those less fortunate, appreciating our many blessings, and taking time for spiritual practices nourish our eternal spiritual nature and help us make the most of our short time on earth.

A grateful attitude about receiving the gift of life is the most powerful statement we can make to God, our children, and our brothers and sisters. One of the most meaningful ways to express gratitude is to help others less fortunate. A Spiritual Capitalist approach to business can ensure you have the income and time to support worthy causes.

Think about those two billion people living on $2 a day. Now, think of all the money you're going to make as a Spiritual Capitalist. It can give you a lifestyle that most never enjoy. I went from a shack with no indoor plumbing to four homes that were architectural masterpieces. I traded a seat in that outhouse for one in a Ferrari.

And then I found the ultimate joy in making big money is helping others. I'm fortunate that I don't need any more money. This book and my speaking engagements are my spiritual mission. I'm setting up a foundation, the Spiritual Capitalist, to help those less fortunate.

When you're enjoying the material comforts that you earned and so richly deserve, while transforming companies and others through love, think about this. The New Testament refers to the poor 800 times. A profound truism that I've experienced is the more I give to and help others, the more I accomplish and the more money I make. Try it. Grace works in mysterious ways.

Count your blessings and gratitude. My mom was right.

## Chapter Summary

- If you maintain an attitude of gratitude you will be more productive and happier in general.

- Most people in the world envy our material blessings and think it must be easy for us to maintain a positive perspective on life. But we just bitch and moan about little bullshit stuff.

- Carry a gratitude list with you defining all your blessings. If you look at your list a couple of times a week and really take it into your heart, you will experience profound transformation.

- A negative, victim-type mind-set will sabotage any chance you have for professional and personal fulfillment.

- The best statement you can make with all the material rewards that come from being a Spiritual Capitalist is helping others.

- My mom was right; she was always right.

# CHAPTER 10

## THE TRUTH WILL SET YOU FREE

*"The truth will set you free."*
*the Bible*

The truth set me free. It took me out of poverty and propelled me into a life of professional and financial success beyond my wildest dreams.

This has been a business book focused on how to take yourself and your company to an optimal level of performance. Going totally against regressive business thought and action, it centers on strong spiritual love as the key in building extraordinary achievements.

As mentioned earlier, when I left the business world, I began studying world religion and theology at Bellarmine University, where I'll also be speaking to the graduate business students about Spiritual Capitalism. Bellarmine is a private Catholic school with a strong spiritual orientation famous for housing the Thomas Merton Center. My dream is that it will become the academic home of Spiritual Capitalism.

A funny thing happened along the way. My thoughts on strong spiritual love became a part of my study, and I saw its universal application. I've come to believe that the ultimate truth is a spiritual issue, and it can set you free in your work and your personal life.

Let me share with you things I learned studying theology and the true spiritual messengers, or masters of the human experience. I saw a significant commonality in all the different faiths and theologies.

## THE SPIRITUAL MASTERS

A spiritually oriented Jungian therapist once told me that when a child is beaten brutally like I was the soul departs because the pain is unbearable. I've always thought this had something to do with my search for spiritual truth.

So I read and studied all the spiritual masters. The Buddha, Moses, Jesus, Confucius, Mohammed, Gandhi, and the great

> *"Spirituality is distinct from institutionalized religion. While religion often looks outward depending on rites and rituals; spirituality looks inward—the kingdom within. Spirituality recognizes that there is something sacred at the core of all existence. Whatever its source, this one sacred element dwells within every living organism. Spirituality is a nondogmatic, nonexclusive, gender-neutral, and nonpatriarchal approach to connect with this one source of all existence. Regardless of our surface differences, there is an underlying sacred commonality. … Dr. Judi Neal, founder and president of the Association for Spirit at Work, has found that managers often confuse spirituality with religion. But, like many others also believe, a person can have an exploration, a deepening of the spiritual experience at work without having people become upset with someone trying to shove a particular point of view down their throat.*
> *Rosner, 2001*
>
> *Journal of the American Academy of Business*
> *Joan Marques, Satinder Dhiman and Richard King*

Hindu master Patanjali. One fundamental truth anchored these masters' philosophy of life. And that truth is love.

Truth is not reserved for Christians or Jews or Muslims or Hindus. It is the universal truth that connects us all.

Once, the great Hindu leader Mahatma Gandhi was asked whether he was a Hindu. "Yes, I am," he said. "I am also a Christian, a Muslim, a Buddhist, and a Jew." Boy, do I love that.

Gandhi once taught "God is truth," but later changed his view to "Truth is God." He characterized truth as a voice inside that defines our own experience and the universe as a whole. He saw the core of every religion as truth and love.

I look at bitter, wired, uptight people and feel a lot of compassion. Many of these people consider themselves "religious." They have an image of God that mirrors their makeup, a God that's judgmental, uptight, and always pissed off about something.

The liberating vision for me is closer to a God in His heaven, reclining on a golden lounge, relaxed and totally at ease. With a mischievous smile on His face, He looks down upon us, His children. He wants us to slow down and smell the roses, to learn to live a life based in love. He knows we're on earth for such a little while and we're here, designed by love, to learn to love.

And if we ask Him about the meaning of life, He'd tells us it is what we make of it.

Think about that. What do you want the meaning of your life to be? What meaning do your actions give it? How do you want others and your God to see you? What legacy will you leave your children? When you face your God in Heaven, how will you feel about reviewing your life on earth? I truly believe that one day we'll discuss all of these issues with our God. Kind of makes you think a bit, doesn't it?

## THE SERVANT LEADER MODEL

Depending on our beliefs and faith, we all look for a model and teacher who can guide us on our personal and professional journey. I referred to some at the beginning of this chapter, all of whom I have tremendous respect for. As a struggling Christian, I happen to look to Jesus of Nazareth.

I see Jesus as one of the greatest leaders who ever lived. Just look at the track record. The impact he had on humanity and our world is breathtaking, especially considering that he started out with only himself and a ragtag handful of followers, most of whom deserted him when he needed them most. He constantly challenged the hypocritical religious establishment.

He loved a good party and to eat, drink, and be merry. Ever see that great picture *The Laughing Jesus*? He loved people. He dined with anyone and everyone and felt a particularly strong sympathy for the outcast and the prostitutes. When the party got dull, he turned the water into wine.

His teachings of "Judge not, that ye be judged" and "Let ye who is without sin cast the first stone" should humble us all and stop that horrible inclination we have to criticize others.

He was arrested by the religious establishment and had his famous encounter with Pilate. With his calm and assured presence, despite the circumstances, he tells Pilate that only truth will set one free. Pilate, with all his power and riches, then asks the ultimate existential question, "What is truth?" That question is what we all must answer to guide our personal and professional lives.

Jesus gave his life for love, and he defined God simply as love personified. With all his vision and courage as a great leader, I am always moved when I think of him taking the bowl of water and washing his disciples' feet, the ultimate symbolism of the servant leader. If this great man could live his life in love and change the world forever, surely we can make the effort to center our words and actions in a loving manner.

## THE SPIRITUAL CAPITALIST PERSPECTIVE

The theme of this book is love in the practice of a spiritually oriented perspective on business. We've talked a lot about what that means.

To change into a Spiritual Capitalist, you need to embrace spiritual truth. Take charge of your life. Decide to live it in truth, so your shackles finally come off and the truth sets you free. This truth is universal, whether you are the CEO of a large corporation, a small business owner, a professor, or somebody who works at Burger King. It crosses all departmental, functional, racial, gender, and socioeconomic lines.

Truth is an ideal to which we should all constantly aspire. Truth is loving yourself, your company, and others. Truth knows you give it your best. Truth means taking responsibility. Truth is a feeling within you about your Creator and this wonderful, crazy, sad, happy adventure we're having together. Truth is about your ability to create a vision of yourself. Truth is knowing you are here for a reason and that reason is to learn how to love and live with truth as a focus in your personal and professional life.

You know how I feel about the textbook, old-school teachings of management, what I call regressive business thought. Those lessons don't work at a quantum level. My school says you can have lots of fun, love, and joy in the workplace and generate incredible financial performance, the best of both worlds. If you're not doing it now, you have the power to reinvent yourself, your people, and your company in a way that empowers you to lead them to the truth.

## THE TRANSFORMATIVE POWER OF LOVE

Remember those questions we asked at the beginning?

What deeply touches us? What moves us to act from our higher self? What motivates us like nothing else?

We all know the answer. It's always been there right in front of us. The most powerful force in our life is love. We know this truth intuitively and experientially. Many have just never developed an awareness of its singular force in our business life.

The essence of my message to you in this book is to integrate this most powerful value into your professional life and see the tremendous benefit it provides in enriching your work environment and stimulating a level of extraordinary performance. As we've discussed, the ultimate act of love in a business context is taking yourself, your team, and your company to that place of self-actualization where true potential is experienced.

Developing a strong sense of spiritual love is an essential underlying principle in life. Our lives can't be neatly compartmentalized into business, professional, personal, play, and family. Life is life. And as my old friend Lionel Richie sang, "Everything in life is about love."

## LOVE IN THE BUSINESS WORLD

So how does the truth of love look in that part of our life we spend in the business world?

Truth is loving yourself, your peers, and your company with actions mirroring this belief. It's taking yourself and others to a level that takes everyone's breath away (I love that phrase) in a culture that nurtures the soul.

It means making the tough decisions, not accepting the unacceptable, and constructively confronting the individual who does not see the light. It means extending yourself for the growth of another. It means being a Spiritual Capitalist.

A lot of people ask what the most powerful and practical steps are in becoming a Spiritual Capitalist. They relate to the concept of developing management as an art and embracing leadership as a sacred responsibility and get it when I talk about the subjects we've discussed.

I like to point out that the latest scientific studies prove that new behavior and thinking literally trigger the neural connections in our brains necessary for genuine change to occur (i.e., transformation in my terms). These studies indicate it should take only about three weeks of consistent effort to start feeling the shift.

If you're truly committed to new behavior and thinking in concert with the Spiritual Capitalist philosophy, we'll look again at the actions that can help you get there:

1. Read, study, and embrace this book and review the Ten Commandments frequently.

2. **Think quantum.**

3. Practice the principles I've given you in this chapter and watch the response.

4. If you can, find a model who exemplifies the Spiritual Capitalist philosophy.

5. **Think quantum.**

6. Put the chart contrasting the Spiritual Capitalist with the Traditional Regressive on your wall.

7. Write a letter to yourself defining who you're going to be and review it frequently.

8. **Think quantum.**

9. Act as if you already are a Spiritual Capitalist.

10. When in doubt, use your internal moral compass—then do what's right.

11. Display a copy of the excerpt from Nelson Mandela's speech in Chapter 2.

12. Review Chapter 1, and decide to make business a spiritual experience and to enjoy all the beautiful benefits this perspective provides.

13. **Think quantum.**

## GETTING TO HEAVEN

I once had someone ask if being a Spiritual Capitalist would help you get to heaven. I think it probably would since it's based on love. But the question led us to one of the spiritual masters for the answer.

One of my favorite discussions regarding Jesus is about heaven. I've heard so much empty rhetoric about heaven and hell that was certainly not about love. It's interesting what comes up when talking with others about heaven and how to get there.

There's only one place in the Bible where Jesus talks specifically about heaven and what you need to do to get there. In fact I see a spiritual metaphor at play when I think about the tired old business model versus one with a philosophy of empowerment, individual liberation, and breathtaking performance (i.e., the company is born again).

Jesus's comments are in Matthew 25 and are at odds with prevailing thought—at that time and this. They center particularly on those of us with many personal, professional, and financial blessings. What are the blessed actions Jesus defines as our road into Heaven? They include:

- Feeding the hungry
- Inviting strangers in
- Clothing the poor
- Helping the sick
- Visiting the prisoners

- Giving the thirsty drink.

The material rewards of the Spiritual Capitalist are plenty, but there is so much more involved. You've earned the riches, the material goodness of life, but you've done it in a way of teaching, caring, and loving others that causes the heavens to unfold for you as you are guided in this noble undertaking by the breath of God. Your journey is one to be honored and admired. It's a journey of transcendence, of being the best human being personally and professionally that you can be.

For me, it's all summarized in our **Ten Commandments of Spiritual Capitalism.**

I.   Define business as a spiritual experience focused on the power of love.

II.  Don't shrink or play small in this world, and recognize your power and presence.

III. Dare to use love by combining the head and the heart to achieve quantum performance.

IV.  Embrace leadership as a sacred responsibility.

V.   Develop management as an art of grace and efficacy.

VI.  Empower your people with genuine psychological, operational, and financial ownership.

VII. Transcend to the higher level above all the BS.

VIII. Don't take it all so seriously, and liberate your true potential in the process.

IX.  Count all your blessings, and construct a foundation of gratitude.

X.   Let the truth within a strong spiritual love provide the path to both personal and professional transcendence, while elevating work into a journey that enhances the meaning of your life.

The truth in the power of love is precious and priceless. It is within you to embrace.

It will set you free.

## Chapter Summary

- The ultimate truth as defined by the spiritual masters is a spiritual issue, and it can set you free in your professional and personal life.

- The transformative power of love is singular and unique.

- The use of spiritual love in a business environment can inspire a rebirth of your company.

- We discussed practical guides in becoming a Spiritual Capitalist.

- Practicing the Ten Commandments of Spiritual Capitalism provides a path to professional and personal fulfillment.

# CONCLUSION

All my literary friends told me that I should have a conclusion for my book. I really don't understand why. If you haven't gotten what I've been talking about by now, I really don't know what else to say. So I'll just leave you, my precious brothers and sisters, with one of my poems—and my love.

# Reflections

As I sit here
Thinking about
The seasons of my life

I see

The women I've loved
The children born

The God I lost
And the God I found

Good friends
Autumn afternoons

The smell of roses
The taste of wine

Yet I wonder about
My life of work

Did I give my best?

Did I touch their lives?
Was I a teacher?
Embracing my students
And showing them the way

To self-transcendence
Fulfillment
To love?

Did I give of my mind?

My heart?
And my soul?

And when I go to Heaven
How will I be judged?

Will the angels soar
In sheer delight?

Will the saints applaud
My every step?

Will the harps salute
With precious sounds?

Will the sun shine?
Will the moon glow?

Will the birds sing?
Will the river flow?

And will my God

Look with love and joy
Upon my soul?

I wonder.

# Michael E. Hendren

*Spiritual Capitalist*

## Author

Michael Hendren is the author of *Spiritual Capitalism: Radical Transformation into Quantum Performance.* A corporate turnaround artist and one of America's highest-paid executives, Michael transformed his last company into the fastest-growing corporation in history at that time, creating a market value of $24 billion in less than six years. What makes this innovator so different is his spirit and compelling love for others. He asserts that corporate rules, policy manuals, and politics kill the soul and hinder financial performance. His seminal business philosophy of Spiritual Capitalism holds the key to quantum financial performance for the corporation and self-actualization for its employees by integrating the mind, heart, and spirit with business acumen. His unique life experience and professional accomplishments underscore the power and efficacy of this breakthrough business strategy.

## Speaker

Michael gives seminars, leads sales meetings, and conducts training programs to transform managers into Spiritual Capitalist leaders. He presents his maverick breakthrough business philosophy in a compelling and dynamic way, inspiring participants to embrace the sacred responsibility of leadership and move their organizations to quantum levels of performance.

## Coach

Michael works individually with CEOs, executives, and sales managers to integrate the Ten Commandments of Spiritual Capitalism into their corporate cultures. He continues with the select group of executives he coaches until they reach the pinnacle of financial performance, professional success, and personal fulfillment.

## On the Internet

Michael's website, www.michaelhendren.com, informs businesspeople who want to transform their lives and organizations radically. The site is updated weekly with articles, case studies, testimonials, videos, and practical applications of Spiritual Capitalism to a wide range of managerial practices.

CPSIA information can be obtained at www.ICGtesting.com
Printed in the USA
LVOW082005200912

299682LV00001B/5/A